# HOLD BA
# THE SPRI

## Fannee Hilander

"There was a time, not so long ago when the five of us had a mother. That was the time when we were blessed with having her, for us all to live and laugh and take for granted. After all, nothing could ever possibly happen to Hash… But as life would have it, something did happen to Hash, and now it is time to remember…"

With these words the author takes us back through the life of her mother, reminiscing with her brothers and sisters in such a personal way that you at times feel impelled to softly close the book and tiptoe away; it is as if you are intruding on memories too personal to share.

*Hold Back the Spring* is a memorial to a wonderful mother, wife and human being. The author presents many memories of the good and the bad times. She presents a book of love, dedicated to keeping alive the memory of her mother.

As the author states: "By writing this book, I have released all the stored up thoughts and emotions for the purpose of preserving her memory."

Although this dramatic true story dwells lingeringly on the subject of death, it might also be called a celebration of life.  Reading of how a daughter deals with the universal subject of losing a parent will surely make each of us cherish our own mothers even more.

# HOLD BACK THE SPRING

To our - Ann
friends,
& Bill !
old friends - are
The best friends ! are
own friendship goes
" way back " ! both
Paypens & I
appreciate you all
so much - Thanks
for your friend-
ship . . . . Love,
Joanne

# HOLD BACK THE SPRING

## Fannee Hilander

TODD & HONEYWELL, INC.
GREAT NECK, NEW YORK/1980

Published by Todd & Honeywell, Inc.
Ten Cuttermill Road
Great Neck, New York 11021

ISBN 0-89962-037-X

Manufactured in the United States of America

# Contents

This book is dedicated to
my sisters, Mary Ann and Alice
and to my brothers, Billy and Lowell.
Also, I dedicate it to
all of "Holly's Pups"—everywhere.

People have always said I lived in a dream world and perhaps I did—it was a nice place to live. Nothing ever went wrong—all my life I was protected and sheltered. The dark side of life I never saw and literally everything turned out right for me.

But my dream world came to an abrupt end as I came face to face with reality outside the intensive care unit at the hospital. The doctor's eyes were telling me the answer to my question even though his words were unsure.

There was no one there but the two of us as I asked him, "Will she live?"...

# HOLD BACK THE SPRING

# 1
# TIMES REMEMBERED

There was a time, not so long ago, when the five of us had a mother. That was the time, when we were blessed with having her, for us all to live and laugh and take for granted. Taking her for granted was not to be considered a fault—that is the way of life. After all, nothing could ever possibly happen to Hash! Maybe to you or me or even to our families—but not to Hash! What an absurd thought! If it should have crossed our mind even briefly, wouldn't we have tossed it aside with all other ridiculous thoughts?

But as life would have it, something did happen to Hash, and now it is a time to remember..........

> Times remembered, words recalled,
> Memories clear and shining.
> Things we did and things she said
> Keep running through my head.
> But days get busy and so do we
> And life seems not so sad.
> But then, in some small quiet corner of my day
> I find her, and I cry.
> But then, I smile and smile
> Because I'm glad she's there.

Before she died, my life was more or less bathed in a golden light. I wasn't prepared for death; her's or anyone else's. It was not a time for dying—there were no signs. Everything was going well and we all had years of life ahead of us.

One summer night, she and James were leaving the farm after having spent a pleasant evening with us. The lights, spaced intermittently down the long driveway, cast shadows around the tall old trees. I hid behind a tree while they turned the car around and as they approached me, I darted out in front of the headlights, then behind a tree, then I ran down the road in front of them like a wild woman. I was barefoot, as I am all summer, and I would jump and scream and flit in and out of the shadows as they winded down the drive. The peacocks were screaming in the trees, startled by my behavior, and Hash was laughing uproarously. She never quit talking and laughing about that "mad woman on the hill." She gloried in moments of silliness—moments of pure foolishness, and so did I.

Before she died, I ran through life like that—carefree and happy—never fearing being hit. I could be in the forefront or the shadows and the shadows held no dread.

But now I have lost that confidence—indeed I have been hit—and the shifting shadows cause me to fear. Life is uncertain and death is never far away; I live on the verge of tears. I can be tumbled into that abyss of tears unexpectedly by one word or fleeting memory; it happens often.

While before I had been trusting and optimistic, I now became cynical; the bottom fell out of my secure little world. Thus began the metamorphosis of my personality and a serious questioning of the philosophy she had taught me: "everything will turn out alright."

All my life, she called me her "Sunshine," and we called her Hash. Not Mother, not Mom—just Hash—short for Hazel. Hash with a long a and how we hated all the different pronunciations of the simple word Hash!

And so, my brothers and sisters, I have written this book as a surprise for you, and I hope it has been the complete surprise I wanted it to be; perhaps you knew all along, but mainly I have written it for myself; it has helped me to come to grips with the reality of her death. Having been attending weekly lectures on how to deal with stress, I told everyone it was so I could help Gadie to deal with his stress. Midway through it, I learned the importance of being honest with yourself, thus I acknowledged the fact that I am going because of my own stress. I am imperfect. I have problems that cause stress. I need help. There—I said it and it wasn't as hard as I thought. Therefore, I have poured my innermost thoughts and feelings into this book of love and it has been absolutely therapeutic!

Alice, remember how you and Mary and I fretted over who would have a nervous breakdown first; if there was to be one apiece, we each wanted to be first. But we three have made it this far since her death; talking and reminiscing together has helped tremendously. But Billy, I worry so about you and Lowell in regard to this grief—do you ever talk about the loss or is it still there inside of you, unable to be released? If in some way this book helps you to break down your feelings to where they can be expressed and analysed, it will have served a purpose.

I want to remember so desperately and I cling to everything I can to preserve her in my memory. That is the reason for this book—to take inventory of my mind. It must be transferred onto paper. The dread of forgetting had consumed me to the point that I had to relive over and over the events leading to her death, trying to contain all that plus the numerous times of her life that were meaningful to me. I felt that I must relive them and in doing so I wouldn't allow even one precious detail to escape me. This, combined with the unbearable sorrow that stays with me, meant that she had taken up permanent residence in my mind. Never do I mean that I want to evict her memory from my mind—never—I just want her image on paper so I can preserve all these precious memories while putting my mind at ease.

This is not in any way meant to present Hash as a saint—Oh, how she would have laughed and laughed at that. No, she wasn't perfect and never pretended to be, but she certainly was a good woman.

So now, as you read, I want you to laugh, I want you to cry—but most of all, I want you to remember..........

# 2
# Hold Back the Spring

Looking forward to the spring is
Something I have always done.
It was a natural thing and as to
Reservations—there were none.
But came last spring, bringing with it
Death and not the life we had expected.
So now all the former joys and delights
Of spring I have rejected.
**Now all the rewards and happinesses**
Which my trek thru life might bring,
I would gladly give up and never regret
If only I could have held back that spring.

Dying is easy, so they say. It's the living that's hard, if you can believe that old song.

I know she's dead. I accept it. I fully believe it...but I just can't comprehend it. It's beyond my understanding for such at thing to be.

It's a terrible thing to lose your mother. You have to feel that golden cord between you severed; it was first severed at birth, but nevertheless it bound you together all your life. When it's cut it's a physical thing that you can actually feel; it's as if a part of you drains away and leaves a great empty space that can never be filled.

I stood with Gadie as he and his sister Ruth held their Mother's hand as she slowly slipped away. It was a terrible thing to see Gadie lose her; she was a fine woman and a good mother.

I saw the great emotional wrench as they were separated; I knew what to expect. But still I wasn't prepared for the empty feeling I had as I looked at Hash—after it was over in the hospital room.

It was quiet and gentle and we softly walked away, one by one, and we will never be the same.

All our life, we have had a mother—now we are motherless.

It reminds me of the saddest day I had with Tracy—before he started school. Bravely we had prepared and talked and hidden our true feelings. School would be fun and exciting. He wanted to go—I was anxious to meet his teacher and see his room—school would be such fun.

Then the night before it started he broke down and cried and he tore my heart out when he said these words; "But I can't leave you! I've been with you all my life!"

That's just the way it was with Hash. It wasn't right for her to go off and leave us like she did. There was nothing right about it.

A woman shouldn't just go off and leave everything behind her—her husband, her children, her friends and her personal things. There should be some warning, some preparation.

All her cosmetics and her trinkets and her clothes, all her books that she loved—they are all still there just as if they were in limbo—awaiting what?

How I dreaded the obituary. When she was at her worse that Sunday, I started realizing that I might actually read such a thing in the paper—that it would be real and not something I could shut out. And then, one day there it was and all my horrible fears were realized. Alice, recently you told me that you have never yet allowed yourself to look at those dark words—that ugly account—that actuality.

On awakening on those mornings, stark reality would strike me like a lightening bolt in that first moment of consciousness..........

I often drive through the cemetery, stopping at her little stone. It gives me a feeling of "going home" and I feel quite at ease there. I feel comforted just to drive through and stop for a minute. I often drive through if I am going somewhere she would have been going with me, like to an assembly or shopping, etc. I suppose it's just as if to say, "I haven't forgotten the things you liked to do."

Tracy and I were so happy to see that the sweet little tulips we planted when the ground was beginning to freeze last fall are starting to push up through the ground. It makes you understand the process of renewal when you see those brave little flowers.

But I feel resentment toward this spring. Can you understand that? Always before, all my life, I welcomed the sweet spring (or early summer as I identified it) with an open heart.

My very first impression of spring was when I was at Mommau's house sitting on my knees and looking out the front window. I could see the little yellow crocus flowers coming up in groups and I heard the grown-ups speak of spring. But it was cold and damp and patches of snow were still around and it took me at least twenty-five years to finally separate the idea of spring from the image of cold and rain.

Literally, until the last five years or so, I couldn't understand why anyone could say spring was their favorite season. Gradually I began to accept the spring as truly a beautiful phase—a beginning..........

But then she went away in the spring, and I cannot feel a warmth toward it ever again. Even now, when sadness comes, for a fleeting second I sometimes am not able to remember what season it is.

> My times of sadness come, as now,
> when the snow falls so very softly,
> covering us all, as it does her, with a
> blanket of purest white, so quiet and gentle.
> It makes my heart hurt,
> but at the same time I am filled with a tranquility
> I do not understand.
> The winter is sad, but maybe not even
> as sad as the spring, when life,
> but not all life bursts forth with exuberance.
> Does spring wonder when she sees the hurt
> in our eyes?
>
> The seasons come and go with regularity;
> we come and go with hesitation.
> I look at this merry-go-round of life
> and I ponder it and I feel resentment;
> then paradoxically I feel a surge of serenity.
> If only I can merge the emotions,
> and bridge the seasons, perhaps
> I can understand the sadness.

On April the eighth she will have been gone a year, two years and then three—I don't want to feel time drifting on past. I want to cling to the freshness of her memory.

How I resent speaking of her in the past tense; my whole being rebels against such a thing. It rebels also against the fact that everyday happenings that I recall have suddenly become cherished memories; "things" of hers are now suddenly "momentos" to cling to.

When you stop to think of it though, every second of each day of each year brings us all closer to the end of life "as we know it now."

When I was in school, my favorite teacher, Mrs. Embry, used to tell us to be aware of the world around us, to look for the beauty in the hidden things. She expected us to report on something we had seen that week, in our surroundings that we hadn't seen before, even though it had been there all along. It's amazing what you can open your eyes to when you truly "look."

Now I tell Scarlett and Tracy to be aware; you can see with your eyes of understanding too, you know.

I tell them to look at the sky each day—really look at it—and not take such a glorious sight for granted. It changes constantly and is a never ending delight—only one of many awesome sights we sometimes look at, but don't really "see." Appreciate life.

Life is precious. Enjoy it now because for each of us it is "slipping away," as it did for her.

The Bible, speaking of our short lives, says: "For it must quickly pass by, and away we fly." That's true, and the same chapter beautifully describes her demise with these words: "we have finished our years just like a whisper."

# 3
# THERE WAS NO WINTER

Her life was, as I see it, divided into approximately three twenty year periods. The first twenty I will appropriately label as spring; the second twenty as summer; the third twenty as fall.

*SPRING:*

The year 1914 was highly important. According to the Bible it was the year the Gentile times ended; the year Satan was cast out of heaven to the vicinity of the earth, and the year Jesus Christ started ruling as King.

It was also the year Fannie Williamson Robertson and James William Robertson had a baby girl named Hazel. She arrived on the ninth day of November.

Little Mary Alice was 10 years old. Although she wasn't sure why, she knew something was wrong when she and the other kids were quickly shunted off to "play" at Aunt Grace's house—at night.

Her sixteen year old brother, Merdie, drove them through the quiet streets of Lexington in a little pony cart. Russell, Tom and Henry, her brothers, went along too and they all played school at Aunt Grace's and ate the fruit she had put out for them. She enjoyed playing with the three cousins until Florence said, "You know, Aunt Fannie is real sick." Then Mary Alice (Bubble) lost all interest in playing and realized why Aunt Grace had left—because Momma was "real sick."

The worrying was over about 11:30 that night when Merdie came back over and announced, "We have a new baby sister!"

So back into the pony cart the little brothers and sisters tumbled and as they rode back down the deserted Main Street, the pony's hoofs beat out the words: a baby sister, a baby sister, a baby sister, a baby sister.

Now, full of anticipation and excitement, they ran into the huge bedroom where a blazing fire was burning in the grate. There they saw Momma lying in the bed with little Hazel on her arm. Momma was happy and laughing and Poppa was in a "big way" too. Now they had another baby girl to fill the terrible void left by the untimely death of little Gertie Lee about six years ealier. She had died when she was about 11 months old. Momma would tell how she would reach for her at night and she was not there; it must be an unbearable hurt to lose a small baby.

Now little Hazel B. could fill their lives and they would pamper and spoil her to their hearts content. And they did. She was the last one of eight children—the baby. Uncle Merdie always called her "Miss Hazel."

Do you know the story of the B, as her middle name? Bubble told it to me. Even though Momma was a submissive wife and let Poppa "rule the roost," she did have her moments when she spoke up and subsequently got her way, albeit in a roundabout way.

The first name she picked because of a little girl across the street named Hazel; the Betty because of her beloved sister Betty. Aunt Betty Sharon—remember?

But Poppa wanted the middle name to be Grace, after his sister Grace who assisted in the birth.

Even though Momma loved Aunt Grace too, she felt enough was enough. Almost all the children had been named after Poppa's "people" and now was the time to assert herself. This she did in a "sneaky" way. She insisted on naming her simply Hazel B. Then as Hash got older, Momma told her the story and Hash "christened" herself Hazel Betty. See how easy it is to get your way?

Poppa was relatively "well-to-do" then, as he was all his life, and Hash led an easy life. Momma always had "help" and there was a good "colored" woman to help after Hash was born. She cooked and did the wash; however, she refused to do the diapers that were "nasty."

Poppa therefore paid Bubble a nickel a diaper to flush the "nastiness" out in the commode before they were given to her to wash. (Ironically, Hash being born in a house with a bathroom had to go full cycle and do without a bathroom after she married until she moved to Etter Lane in 1960.)

She lived there on South Upper Street for about two years. Here she played with Henry (Uncle Pal) and Russell whom she adored greatly. She always told me what "fine" young men they were and how respectful they were. She would lie for hours, listening to them reciting poetry, storing it up in her mind. It was inculcated in her to such an extent that it made a lasting impression.

Mary Ann, remember the family reunion we had at the farm in 1978? Nelson sat at the table beside the pool with Uncle Pal and Glenne and Bubby and they exchanged lines and snatches from poems, seeing who could remember the names and authors of the various ones. That's when Nelson realized what "a gentleman and a scholar" Uncle Pal really was. He has a love of words and also enjoys a play on words. Hash did too; I miss her so much when I need to know about a word. I would run to the phone and call her and what a simple pleasure that was—to have her as close as the phone. I miss her so.

She loved Uncle Pal and had a great rapport with him. Bubble has the sweetest picture of her standing beside him and he was dressed in knickers and a little flat cap. Hash told me how they used to run to the library together and lose themselves in the magic of books. She never ever lost that fascination for books. I wonder what she would think of this one. Would she be embarrassed, flattered or honored.........

Momma dressed her in little dark gingham dresses and she had her hair cut (or bobbed) straight across. To me it seemed to have an oriental look, from the pictures I have seen. Aren't pictures the most wonderful thing? I fully appreciate pictures. Word pictures are nice too.

Bubble didn't like the little old fashioned dresses Hash wore; she knew Momma just didn't know any other way to do it. So she looked through a catalog and picked out a sweet little pale blue one and a pale pink, and Momma was glad to pay for them. Later Bubble bought her a beautiful velvet dress, and she would pull her to church on a small sled.

When she was eight she surprised her with her hearts desire—a pair of roller skates! How she loved them! Momma wasn't too enthused with them, but she allowed it.

Hash attended Ashland School. At various times Poppa had grocery stores. They were located at different places: Georgetown Street, Second Street, Upper, South Lime, and two at Muddy Ford.

I have picked Bubble's mind for stories and anecdotes on Hash when she was young. At nine months she walked and was always active. She told me about her doing something to aggravate Momma and when Momma tried to catch her to spank her, she climbed up on some boxes in the store where she couldn't reach her. Then she sat there, swinging her legs back and forth, and grinning, as if to say "catch me if you can!"

Around the corner from the store lived a sweet old man and woman. They were black, and Hash loved them, as they did her. She would wander off from the store and when Momma missed her, she would send Bubble off to find her. Without fail she would be located at the old couple's house, sitting up in a high chair, eating with them. Life was slow then—people were good. No speeding cars to run down a child; no molesters to worry about.

When she was about three years old they moved to the store Poppa had on Limestone—I believe he had seven stores in all. Poppa was always a character—larger than life it seemed. He was known all through the country and was recognized as a great practical joker. Everyone knew Willie Robertson—some knew him as J.W. Robertson.

His life would require a book in itself, therefore I won't dwell at length on his escapades. Here however, are two little examples of his humor and wit.

There was a parade in town and at the end of the parade came the elephants. There were several of them and each one held the tail of the one in front in its trunk. They were trudging awkwardly down the street and when the last one passed in front of Poppa's sister—Aunt Lizzie Mallory—she gasped out: "Good Lord, there's Willie!!" Poppa had fallen in line, holding the tail of the last elephant and making a perfect spectacle of himself in front of his prim sister.

The other incident involved a visit he and his brother Arthur made to the state asylum to see someone there.

When the time came to leave and they were waiting for the guard to open the gates, Poppa turned to Uncle Arthur, patted him on the shoulder and told him to go on back in and he would be back to visit him whenever he had a chance. The guards wouldn't allow Uncle Arthur to follow Poppa out; they listened to Poppa's explanation that his brother was thoroughly confused and Uncle Arthur's futile explanation only helped convince them.

So in this fine atmosphere of wit and poetic expression Hash grew into her young womanhood. She was perhaps overly protected and sheltered as only a young lady with four older brothers should be. Added to this was the indulgence of an older sister who pampered her and did all the work assigned to Hash rather than have her do her share. Bubble told me she would jump up and do the dishes or anything else Momma told Hash to do; she said Hash could do all that sort of thing when she got older.

Clothes were a passion with her and quite easy to attain. All she had to do was to convince Momma that she "desperately" needed a certain dress and Momma would intercede between her and Poppa. She would get the dress.

Often she described dresses and coats she used to wear; they stuck in her mind and seemed to be unusually beautiful things. (She wore princess style dresses of beautiful colors and materials, fitted coats with lavish furs around the collar and hats and tams to match. Do you even know what a tam is?)

I've seen pictures of her at that age and her self-confidence and flirtatious nature fairly emanated from the print.

She was indeed the Bell of the land when Poppa had the store at Muddy Ford. She had boyfriends galore and she told me of the many different proposals of marriage she had. Since she died, I have had numerous people come up and tell me what a beautiful girl she was. Some have even said she was "the most beautiful girl they ever saw."

Along with these qualities came a temper and an excitable nature. One of the few times, and perhaps the only time she ever had a skirmish with Poppa, was witnessed by Bubble. Whatever the occasion, she had worked herself up into a frenzy and even screamed out at Poppa. Now that was not to be done—it was completely out of line! Bubble, the ever present protector, knew something had to be done to prevent a calamity, so she did what was necessary. She slapped Hash in the face, and immediately she got control of herself. Better a slap than to be be-headed or disowned or something even worse!

Jesse Sharon, her cousin and best friend through all those girlish years shared many experiences with her.

One time a boyfriend came unexpectedly, catching Hash and Jesse in the midst of a forbidden cigarette! Before she went to greet him, Hash snatched up a bottle of perfume and gargled it! Shades of Scarlet O'Hara, but years before the movie.

Another time, full of mischief and boredom, they dared each other to toss a shoe full of—pardon the indelicacy of this—urine out the upstairs window, just to see if it might hit someone passing by on the sidewalk!

When she was sixteen, she often helped Poppa in the store. A cantankerous old woman came in with eggs to trade for her groceries and she irritated Hash so in the process of making her count and recount the eggs that Hash became completely exasperated. She ran into the house, which adjoined the store, and demanded a butcher knife from Momma to "do away" with that "dispisful" old woman! She never did like "dispisful old women."

Speaking of old women, there was an old "colored" woman who was sitting on her porch near the store and she stopped Hash as she was playing nearby to ask a favor of her. Hash was probably roller skating on the sidewalk, as that was her favorite pastime. The old lady said, "Honey, will you take this money and run over to the store and get me a spool of thread? I'm tied." Hash ran into the store, all out of breath, and announced there was old lady tied up on the front porch and for someone to go get her loose! (the old lady was *tired*)

Oxford School figured highly in our lives. Hash and Daddy both graduated from there; Gadie and I both went there. Kay and Aunt Ann taught there.

I often dream about things happening in the old familiar hallways and rooms. Gadie regretted that he didn't buy it when it was at auction several years back, for sentimental reasons only. Otherwise it would be practically worthless. Remember the gym and the balcony overlooking it? I loved that old balcony that ran the length of the gym. It had old dark oiled floors and it was two levels.

So in May of 1934 she graduated and then three and a half years later she was married, breaking a lot of hearts along the way. Some people seemed surprised that she married Daddy. Several years ago a woman told me that she never was so surprised in her life when she heard that Hazel and Woodrow were getting married.

But others in the family were not surprised and they approved of and liked "Daddy." He was from a good respectful family, well thought of in the community, and just back from some learnin' at Eastern College. She was the "girl of his dreams" and after all, they had been "childhood sweethearts," as Daddy said.

He would walk down to see her, as he lived then on the same farm you live on, Bill. During their courtship, Daddy said he regarded her as an "angel" and he put her on a "pedestal" where she belonged.

And so they were married on December 31, 1937. She was twenty-three and Daddy was six months older. They were married at Bubble's house about 4 o'clock in the afternoon; Aunt Ann and Uncle Joe stood up with them. Hash wore an "Alice blue gown" and appropriately her Uncle John performed the ceremony.

Uncle John offered to have his three daughters, Alice, Mary and Mildred, sing "I Love You Truly," but Hash didn't seem to want any music or anything at all to prolong the wedding. That's the way she was; she disliked any "pomp and ceremony" in connection with herself.

Then Bubble fixed a little supper for all of them while they went to visit Uncle Merdie and Aunt Mable. Thus ended the springtime of her life.

## SUMMER:

The early days of their marriage were spent at Daddy's home on the hill with Mommau and Poppau—Mary Morris and Henry Clay Fields. They were fine people; they were good decent people. I always think of Poppau as such a quiet, gentle person. In my memory, he is very dim, fading into the shadows, as indeed he was doing in actuality at the time. He was dying from tuberculosis, and I can remember him in bed as different ones softly looked in on him.

I have no memory of him being up and around but I have some of Mommau's memories of him and some of Kay's. They called him Dad, and Kay told me how she was such a tomboy and how she would ride everywhere Dad went, perched behind him on a horse.

I remember Hash telling me that after supper Poppau always liked to sit out on the porch awhile and would ask Mommau to come out too. However, she always wanted to clean up the kitchen first and by the time she was through and taking off her apron to come out, he was usually ready to go to bed. That always seemed sad to me.

That porch, in the evening, was truly a pleasant place. Nothing has ever sounded as melancholy and lonesome as those whip-poor-wills calling to one another after dark. Mommau would rock Billy in the swing and wrap her apron around him to ward off the chill that came up from the valley.

I believe I would give a thousand dollars to have whip-poor-wills out here at the farm to listen to at night and to shiver at the old lonesome sound.

Then Poppau died and I can vividly recall someone, probably Daddy, holding me in his arms as we looked down into the casket.

After that, Mommau went on as usual, but even as young as I was, I knew she missed him desperately..

She had a habit of setting the table at night, after she had done the supper dishes, in readiness for breakfast. She turned the plates upside down over the silverware. I could sense her sadness as I saw her set Poppau's plate every night just as if he had never gone away.

So the newly-weds lived with Mommau and Poppau awhile, then they were asked to come back down to Momma and Poppa's to live because of Poppa's health.

Following a sick spell, he needed to take a rest in the afternoon, so Hash would watch the store then and while he ate his meals.

They lived in the "back room," and being there at home, life must have gone on somewhat the same as before.

Late one night while they lived there Hash and Daddy both got an overwhelming urge for hamburgers; not wanting Momma and Poppa to know of this foolishness, they slipped out a back window and drove to town. To me this is sad because it is one of the only really "frivolous" things I ever heard of them doing together.

So then almost a year and a half after she married she began to flower out in motherhood—her first "blossom" being little Lowell Scott.

She adjusted well to motherhood—it came quite naturally. Of course she was living at home with Momma, sweet patient Momma, who had plenty of help and advice for her I am sure.

For a certainty, Momma must have cautioned her on the proper way to handle a baby and the fact that babies are not play things. Earlier, when Barbara was a tiny baby, Hash and Aunt Bea would actually toss her back and forth like a little bean bag!

After your birth, Lowell, Hash was determined to be in a place of her own, and they moved away from Momma and Poppa's to the "Houston Place."

Daddy went to Lexington and bought a "brand new cook stove," then he and Hash went back to the store to buy what they needed to "set up housekeeping." Potatoes, flour, beans—all the staples were piled into a washing tub, along with a sparkling new washboard!

Before now, Poppa would never accept any money for rent or food from Daddy. He would say, "Whiz Fire, I don't want your money. You all do enough work around the store to take care of it." Being as affluent as he surely was, and in the habit of carrying almost all of Muddy Ford on credit until the yearly tobacco crops were sold, he spurned Daddy's offer of payment.

Now after Hash had gathered up everything she needed, Daddy made a broad sweeping gesture and grandly announced, "Now just double the whole order." Poppa did as he was told, after which Daddy proudly paid for the whole thing, probably much to Poppa's surprise.

Momma didn't teach Hash to cook; Hash didn't teach me to cook; I *must* teach Scarlett to cook!

When I first got married, my first meal (setting the pattern for years to come) was fried chicken. I washed the chicken (I guess) and put it directly into the oil in the skillet. Finally I realized why it looked so—strange—I had left off the flour!

Hash cooked hominy—for the first time. She poured it into the boiling water just like the directions said—only she poured the whole box full in! Daddy was with her and first they had a pan full, then two pans full and so on! Oh well, so much for the joys of cooking.

So life went on. Daddy had two tobacco crops and he would walk from the Houston Place to Mommau's and get the team of horses up and work in the fields. Hash took care of Lowell and kept house and then before long it was time for me to come along—December 30, 1941. I was born in the John Graves Ford Memorial Hospital in Georgetown. I was named after Momma.

At six months I took the whooping cough and they tell me I almost died. That must have been a terrible time for Hash, otherwise life seemed quite uneventful and normal.

Then one day Lowell went splitting the gravel down to Momma's house, really tearing up the road. Bubble happened to be there and responded to his distress signals, taking him home to see why Hash was so distraught.

Hash was still young and still spoiled to a certain degree and Hash had just realized she was pregnant!

Bubble calmed her down and quieted Lowell and me, and eventually realized the reason she was so distressed was mainly because the whole house was full of dirty clothes and the old washing machine was broken! Enough to send any woman off her rocker, wouldn't you agree?

Bubble gathered up all the clothes (and probably the kids) and took them to the cleaners, thereby restoring order to both the house and Hash's disposition. She said that after that Hash never minded being pregnant— she was happy about it. But she just couldn't stand mayonnaise.

Around that time we moved to Lexington where Daddy took on a job at General Telephone, working on the lines. Our house was rented from a lady that I always associated with a witch, named Mrs. Lake. Looking back, I'm sure I must have heard Hash speak of her as "that old witch," therefore, the connection in my mind.

It was a double house, the other side being occupied by the landlady herself. There was no love lost on Mrs. Lake; she seemed to be one of those "dispisful old women."

There must have been a black iron fence around the yard because now when I see a fence like that with little spikes on top, I inevitably think of Mrs. Lake and being little. Also, only if I see a fence like that in Lexington—in no other town do I make a mental connection.

Bubble and Shelia lived close by and Bubble said they would come over about every day. Bubble would take Lowell and Shelia would get me out of the baby bed and they would take us out for a walk. Being pregnant, Hash was extremely grateful for the help.

Shelia was young and unmarried and she gave me the love and affection she had stored up. She has told me that at that time, before she knew motherhood, that she said she could never love one of her own as much as she did me.

Shelia is such a sweet, good person, and I love her dearly. Now she has her own children, Vonnie and Mac, to lavish that love on, plus Chip, Chris and Josh.

Daddy had a good job working for the telephone company. We probably were happy there thought I have no rememberance of living there, not even vaguely. I wish I could remember back that far, but I was only two.

Not long ago, I sat and listened to Daddy as he mentally sorted out "the pieces of his life." He commented that "if" he had stayed with that job he would have soon been promoted to a higher position and would have had an excellent opportunity for a better life and things might have been so much different.........

However, he said he was needed and was asked to come back "down to those hills where I worked my ass off for years for nothing."

Immediately this is what came into my mind: "Of all the words of pencil and pen, the saddest are these—it might have been."

So back we came to Muddy Ford to the "Cox Place." I remember it quite well—some details are even vivid. I can recall how the house looked as we would be coming home; I can see it there with the big old front porch—just waiting for us.

Remember that classic picture of Hash and some of us kids sitting on the porch steps and the old hen that wandered into range just in time to be included in the picture?

Under that porch, while the grown-ups talked above us, we played in the dark coolness. How fine and dark the dirt was—it was a marvelous place to play.

And now it was time for a new baby to come along—Mary Ann—circa December 18, 1943. So now I was blessed with a new playmate—a playmate for life.

"Miss" and Ira Sutton, two good old folks, lived across the road and they always seemed glad to have us visit. There was an old cellar before you went in the house and I can remember it so well. In the house, I always seemed to sit in the same place—it was a little couch in front of the fireplace and on the mantel was a weather device of some sort. It may have been a clock and on one side an old mean witch would come out if the day was cloudy; Hansel and Gretel would come out if it was sunny. How utterly fascinating that was to me; I could (and probably did) watch it for hours. Then "Miss" would fix me a cornbread muffin with jam on it and how I relished every morsel.

Hash said they would just beg her to bring us over to visit them; old people get so lonely and kids make the day not quite so long.

"Miss" would be sewing and Hash always "marveled" (privately to us, not to "Miss") over the tiny pieces of leftover thread she would bother with threading and using. They were no longer than this: _____ _____and she would actually use them. Some old folk are extremely frugal. Some have to be.

Once I was with a group of young people from the church at Muddy Ford and we went to their house and stood outside the door singing songs. It was a surpise to them and they opened the door and came out on the porch with such happy expressions on their faces. I can still see them standing there, she with her hands clasped over her little apron and I believe he was leaning on a cane. They seemed so touched and pleased.

Not long ago, I happened to see two little old graves, side by side, at the cemetery. Printed on them were the names of "Miss" and Ira. Pausing for a few minutes there, a flood of memories came back to me—memories of a little old woman and her husband who seemed perfectly content to sit by the fire and be together. And they were kind to children.

I think it was at this house that "Wavy Bell" used to visit us. She was a teenage neighbor girl and would come by often. I don't know her last name, but she once asked Hash: "Why in the world would you name a child Fannee??" Hash, being too nice to make the reply to her that she wanted to, saved it for us later. She asked of us the obvious question "Why in the world would anyone want to name a child Wavy Bell??"

I think, but I'm not sure, she was the one who had her brother and sister hold the kitchen door closed so Hash wouldn't come in while she got Zesta crackers out of our cupboard. Hash was so indignant when she snapped: "I would have gladly given them all the old stale crackers in there, but they didn't have to sneak them out like that!"

I remember being very small and being dressed daintily in pinafores every day and white shoes. (Do I actually remember that part or do I remember the numerous pictures of me—always in little white starched pinafores?)

Lowell, you and I played together every day; Mary Ann was still a baby. Hash would fix us both a little tin lunchbox full of "goodies" and we would play around the cellar. I can see that, I can feel how I felt then— vividly.

Once when I came in from play, I was still clean and my pinafore was still dainty, but the contents of my pockets sent Hash into a fit of laughter. I had picked up all the little black shiny "sheep turds" my pockets would hold! She told that story often to people and always laughed about it.

Now it is 1945 and "along comes Bill"—William Clay to be exact. His birth must have been tinged with sadness for Daddy because as one new life began, one other life was ebbing lower each day—Poppau's.

Bill, they carried you in for Poppau to see as soon as you were brought home from the hospital and he held you in his arms while lying in bed. A generation comes and a generation goes.......... On Novemer 2, 1945 Poppau died.

Now we moved in to be with Mommau so she wouldn't be alone. We moved to the familiar old white house on the hill; it was the one that felt like home. I'll always love it there. The house with the white rock wall covered with rambling roses, the pear tree, the swing in the back, the chicken house........

While we lived there, Hash and Daddy would get up in the middle of the night and start making chocolate pies! Daddy would do the filling and Hash the crust. I don't remember if there was any left for us in the morning; surely they didn't wake us in the middle of the night. Let sleeping dogs lie........away from the pie.

Kids always like to pick on their mother's pretty cake, don't they? And mothers don't want them to; they warn them to leave the cake alone until time to cut it. Hash loved to tell how I was just "going to town" on her cake once when her head was turned. I was about four years old and I would tell her "I won't bother your cake Hash, cause I'm too precious." Can you believe it—I should have been beaten with a stick!

Vividly I recall swinging in a tree in the backyard. It isn't there anymore. It was winter and I was all bundled up and my hands were practically frozen to the rope; it was wonderful!

Hash asked me if I liked swinging in the winter, and I said I liked it even better than the summer. She couldn't believe that, and even as I was saying it I knew I didn't really mean it either. I must have been expecting her to tell me to come in, that it was too cold to be out. Back then I was already trying to rationalize on things that I knew didn't even make sense; sometimes I still do.

I was always happy in my childhood. I have nothing but good memories or I should say with the exception of such a few bad ones that they can easily be tossed to the side of my mind, out of sight. But I guess I'd have to say that the happiest I, or we, ever were was when we made our next move to the little house "up the hollor" behind Kay and Lindsay's house. To me and to my simple child's mind at the time, life was perfect. I loved it there.

The house escaped being called a "rundown shack" by the very fact that it eluded a certain ageless dignity that accompanies the tired grace of an old log cabin. Old it was; tired it was. Boards had given up, like old bones, creaking with age until they finally collapsed and fell, unnoticed.

The massive chimney on the side, surely once a monument to the house, had succumbed to the elements of the years, crumbling slowly. However, a transformation took place once the rooms were filled with "a real live family." The old house came alive; it seemed to smile.

By day, as we romped and squealed, it's walls seemed to expand to accommodate five rowdy kids; at night, when all was quiet and the coal-oil lamps were lit, (the electricity wasn't hooked up until a few weeks later) it's windows shone with a golden glow.

Outside, close to the back porch door, the peach tree hung heavy with fruit, the apple trees were on a little knoll, ready for the picking. Lilacs and honeysuckle bloomed, as if for the first time; tricycles and stick horses appeared out of nowhere. The old house was now a home.

Charles (Reeves) did so many good things for us when we were little. I'll never forget how kind and generous he was to us. Remember the tricycles he gave us? Now most people would have given you one or maybe two tricycles, but not Charles! Each one of us kids got one—ranging in size from tiny to bicycle size! I'll never forget how absolutely thrilled we were and how Charles laughed that big distinctive laugh of his and seemed to get as much "kick" out of it as we did, just by seeing the amazed expression on our faces.

Remember the steep little stairway that led to our play room upstairs? Daddy used to point out to people that the door had wooden pegs (or hinges)—a real attestment to its antiquity.

There was the first room you entered with it's door leading into the tiny little room beside the chimney—then there was the middle room with the huge rock chimney which covered the whole wall! At least it was that way in my mind; how vividly I could see it! But this spring when we all took a trek up there to relive old memories, after a picnic at Kay's, to my dismay I found that the huge fireplace had, shall we say, shrunk? It was considerably smaller than what I remembered it to be. But I too am a different size than what I was then; perhaps that is the answer.

Then the next room was the kitchen. There used to be a little bird that came to the window all the time—we'd put crumbs out for it.

The screened-in back porch ran the length of the last two rooms and that was it.

One night I walked out on the back porch and to my amazement I saw a perfect cross over the moon. Hash and Daddy ran out when I called and they stood in complete silence, looking. The spell was broken when Daddy opened the screen door and looked out. The screen had formed an illusion of a cross, causing some mighty weird feelings on our part.

I thought about God a lot when I was that age. I remember going around the house, outside that kitchen window, and laying a little bouquet of wild flowers, dandelions and violets, on a certain spot. I decided if they were gone when I went back at a determined time, that was a sign that there was a God who knew what I was thinking. I went back to that spot this Spring and tried to remember if they had been gone or not when I checked..........

There is so much to remember—so much to say. Word pictures are nice but in no way can they convey the warm feeling of intimate memories tucked "between the pages of my mind."

I plan to paint a picture of the little house soon; I will paint it the way it used to be. And coming out of the corner of one window, one eye, so to speak; I will paint a tear.

Poppa always ran a grocery store, and he had several of them destroyed by fire. You might say the last fire destroyed him too.

I was staying all night with Shirley the night it happened. Up in the night we heard Aunt Bea call out, "Fire, Fire!" Shirley and I tumbled out the door into the night before we realized it was not their house that was on fire!

Poor little Momma came and sat on the front porch; Aunt Bea put a blanket around her while Poppa stood in the yard with a lot of the neighbors, watching, just watching. It was too late to do anything else.

My little raincoat with the hood was hanging on their wall; I had left it down there the night before.

Good friends always rally to help one another and this was true in

Momma and Poppa's case. They had many friends. Mr. Willie and Miss Fannie were well liked and indeed loved by many people. Words were appreciated, but now a place to live was needed, and this was supplied by Mr. and Mrs. Cummins who were not using their furnished house, which was just about two miles from us. How glad we were to have them near!

After going to church on Sunday at Mt. Gilead, we would catch a ride over with the R.B. Gregg's family to spend the rest of the day with Momma and Poppa. They lived directly across the road from the Greggs and Delores and Judy were the ages of Mary Ann and me. One time their mother made chocolate ice cream and asked us to come over and eat some and I remember how delicious it was.

Speaking of going to church reminds me that Momma and Poppa hardly ever went. It is said that Poppa, as a young man, put his clothes on wrongside out and rode a horse through the church! Can you imagine— don't you love it?! He was the biggest character in the whole countryside! The original protester! A man of truth.

Hash was now pregnant with her last child. I can't remember her pregnancy; I just remember my ecstasy at the marvelous prospect of having a real live baby to play with like a doll!

"Keep a stiff upper lip and a tight A-hole." This graphic encouragement was found on a card to Hash from Bubble during the last stages of one of her pregnancies. I'm not sure which pregnancy this referred to; I found it in the cedar chest. Fortunately Hash always had Bubble there to build up her morale when she was pregnant as well as to build up a collection of baby gowns and diapers and blankets, etc. That was something good old Bubble always did—helped to have things ready for the little new-borns, and how it was appreciated.

Coming into Hash's house late one night, more than slightly inebriated, Lowell was surprised to find Bubble in the bed he had headed for. His heart-felt, fuzzy soliloquy as overheard by Hash included these lines: "She looks just like a big angel laying there. I'll love her til the day she dies."

Don't you just love that story? And indeed that summed up my own feelings for Bubble. The childhood picture my mind retains is one of her in a big fur coat coming up the walk to the house with her arms outstretched.......always.

To me the prospect of a baby almost equaled the joy that having a pony would bring. I used to sit and daydream about having a pony to ride all over the country and now the second best thing came about—a baby. It was you, Alice Dean, born July 13, 1949.

When Hash brought you back, you had on a long white gown, and I got to hold you and I could hardly contain myself. It was not to be believed.

Now when Scarlett and Tracy occasionally beg me to have a baby so they can hold and play with it, I remember and I can feel what they feel.......

It was hot July and you were newborn and Poppa wanted to have a celebration in honor of the event. He and Momma walked from the

"Cummins Place" to our house. He carried a large watermelon all the way. And Poppa was 76 years old.

Sometimes the next week, in the middle of the night, Poppa had a stroke. Momma ran through the darkness and crossed a narrow bridge, it seemed like a swinging bridge, to call for help from the Greggs. The doctor came, and the family was called in. Bubble came from Lexington immediately to tend him as she had done every time before. She had been with him through every sickness and operation; she was the one he depended on and wanted with him.

Now the house was hushed and quiet. The family was all there. The grandchildren were taken in one by one to stand by his bed for a moment. In no way did I grasp the significance of what was happening; I was only six and a half years old.

All her married life Momma had been well taken care of by Poppa. He protected her from life, amused her with his rambunctious ways and together they had enjoyed the love and respect heaped upon them by their offspring.

Now, about 53 years later, it was time for Poppa to leave her and we saw Momma's heart break in two.

The ambulance came to take him to the hospital and we were all in the yard. He was propped up in the back of the open doored ambulance, waving to us as they slowly drove out of the yard.

Even though her children were all around her to offer comfort, I can still remember clearly how small and all alone Momma looked, as she broke down and cried as she tried to wave goodby to Poppa. She would not see him again.

Lowell, Mary Ann and I got off the bus from school and Kay stopped Mary Ann and me but let Lowell go on by. She said: "Tell Hazel that your Grandpappy has died." But she cautioned us not to let Lowell know till he got home or as she said: "He'll kill himself getting there."

Thankfully, we didn't have to be the ones to break the news to Hash because Uncle Tom and Aunt Bea and Shirley were already there.

Being so excited to have Shirley there, my very favorite cousin, I was anxious to have her run out and play with me. I felt slightly puzzled when she admonished me with these words: "Fannee Gayle, don't you understand, Poppa's dead." Yes, it was true—Mr. Willie, who often told his friends, "I hope I live forever and you never die" was indeed dead.

However, he faced death with the same living hope of a resurrection that Hash had and won't they be delighted to see it all come true in due time?

People came from everywhere for Poppa's funeral; it was the largest ever held at Johnson's Funeral Home at that time.

A sad little drama was played out at the time. Glenne and Bubby were driving through Georgetown on their way home from a vacation and upon seeing the large crowd at the funeral home, overflowing into the yard, they idly wondered what important person had died. Imagine their consternation when they recognized Uncle Merdie standing among the crowd; only then did they learn the sad news.

So now Hash had a new baby and had lost her father. I don't know how she reacted—I wish I did. Our life went on as usual. In the summer the days stretched out forever and they were filled with simple joys: wading in the surrounding creeks, swinging from grapevines, riding old Dolly and Bess, picking blackberries to sell, climbing the high sycamore trees and running in and out of Kay's house.

Kay was always good to us; we could depend on her for anything. She was "there" and we knew it. It meant a lot. She had planned to take "us kids" to see the movie, "Uncle Toms' Cabin" one weekend. The fact that the day brought one of the worse snow storms of the winter didn't deter her one iota; nothing ever did stop her, then or now, "so we struck out" in her little coupe. Coming to a certain steep hill which was completely iced over, we all got deathly quiet, holding our breath, wondering if the little car would make it. It did, and only then did we dare to breathe! Kay had brought us through! Hurrah!

Then came the fall and we were all through the thickets and bushes in pursuit of walnuts, persimmons and pawpaws. How strange that our kids today hardly know what we are talking about when we mention pawpaws. Not that they were much to miss, don't get me wrong, but they were there and it was something to do.

This spring I saw an ad for a pawpaw tree in a nursery book and eagerly I ordered it, anticipating my delight in showing Scarlett and Tracy this long lost fruit.

I anxiously watched it grow and to my chagrin, in the late summer, it bloomed out in red flowers; it was a Rose of Sharon bush. I had ordered it at the same time! Only one order had come, with no explanation, and why I assumed it was the pawpaw tree I do not know. So now my children may never taste the delights of a ripe pawpaw and is not that a blessing in disguise?

Then came the winter and the little potbellied stove seemed to be ready to burst with its efforts, rising splendidly to the occasion of warming us and keeping the ever present pot of beans or vegetable soup simmering.

We would fight with snowballs and ride dishpans down the hillsides and skate precariously on the thin iced ponds.

Through the days, through the seasons, through the years, can you remember what Hash was doing while we were doing the above mentioned things?

She was reading. Reading and cooking. Cooking and reading.

Reading must have been the ultimate escape for her—how she loved books! She got them from the library, from Dorothy Houston and from wherever else she could. She would curl up on the couch—remember that studio couch—with her feet tucked away. She could never stand for her feet to show—she said she had the ugliest feet in the world. She was mistaken though.

Now I marvel at the fact that she never worried about us! She seemed totally unconcerned about any danger that we might have been exposed to, which must have been considerable. There was water and animals and heights that we confronted daily in our quest for childish adventure. And we were foolhardy and reckless at times.

With Scarlett and Tracy, for instance, I don't worry excessively, but I am always, and I mean always, aware of where they are and of what they are doing. If Scarlett is in the barn working with her horse, I am thinking about that, and if a reasonable length of time passes without her emerging, I am over there checking on her or having someone else do so. If Tracy is riding a lawnmower or some other vehicle, I watch him intermittently through the window; likewise I listen for Gadie when he is on a tractor.

In retrospect, I wonder how we ever escaped serious injury at some time or another. We were completely on our own, weren't we? Billy, your broken arm was the only calamity I can recall. You were swinging on a low rail in the barn and fell, didn't you?

We used to run across the top rails of the barn and even play tag up in there! What in the world would we do if we saw our kids doing that? I would immediately chalk it up as either a serious lack of intelligence or a self-destructive attitude, yet we had neither of those motives or excuses; we were simply running wild and having fun doing it.

We rode down a hill inside of a tire. Lowell, you built a raft out of old doors and went into very deep water. We pulled an old tobacco wagon to the top of a steep hill and had a hair-raising ride down to the bottom. We got on top of buildings and would swing to the ground from tree branches and we jumped into haystacks without first checking for pitchforks. We lived dangerously. We survived gloriously—and surprisingly.

We were ready to leave our little house and move back to the "old home place" on the hill. Not a "mansion on the hill," but considerably better than where we were. The move was deemed necessary because Mommau could no longer live there alone. For quite some time we children had been taking turns staying with her; it was now time for a move. As the last truckload of furniture and children rumbled slowly away, the little house was once again left alone. Quiet and deserted. Kay says that it has been considered for the National Registry of Historic Houses; how I hope something is done about it before it is too late. It deserves to be remembered.

Recently I mentioned to Gadie how I hated to see it crumble and disappear, as old houses surely do, and he said he would gladly buy it and transfer it to our farm if Kay would sell it. If so, I would restore it, and furnish it with the type of furniture we had. I would hang pictures of us, as we were then, on the wall and it would be a labor of love.......

We were happy and carefree at Mommau's too. I remember how we played. My, how we played! There was no TV—no phone and we didn't go many places—so we played together.

We played "cowboys" by the hour in the back of the house. That was always your suggestion, Lowell.

Remember the screened-in back porch that was Mommau's kitchen? What a pleasant place that was. I dream about it often, last night in fact. There on the outside of the windows which ran the length of the room, were the most glorious grapevines. Huge purple, juicy grapes, the likes of which I will never find again. We played in and out of those vines like mice, climbing ladders which we had half concealed in the vines and running little cars along the bottom ledge.

My favorite game was "Bombi." He was the equivalent of Tarzan I suppose—he was a jungle boy. I almost always got to be "Bombi." If I didn't get to be him, I wasn't "in the mood" to play.

Once, in a daring escape from my captors, I leaped off the chicken house roof to the ground which was very far down. It is a great wonder that I didn't break every leg I had, but amazingly I escaped unharmed. That made me really big in everyone's eyes. I was a hero, and probably got to be "Bombi" from then on.

I can still remember the high excitement of being flattened against the wall, partially concealed by the grapevines and out of breath from the chase as the rest of you passed by just inches from your prey, on through the rainy darkness, searching, searching....

I won't allow Scarlett and Tracy to play out in the darkness, except at the farm where we are fenced in from the world. It's a shame, but in town you have to be wary of the shadows in the far reaches of the yard, the corners where the light doesn't shine. People are strange. But we could play out anytime, every night. Hash didn't care and she didn't worry.

But one time she said "no". It stands out vividly in my mind because she just didn't say no, at least not to me. But this time she did, and she said it so firmly that I knew she meant it. Of course, it would have been much better had she said "no" more often on things; that was a fault and not a virtue. What a great difference there is between the way she was so permissive and I am so restrictive. No happy medium. But too much freedom is definitely not good and I am sure of that.

Now you are anxious to know what she refused me on, aren't you?

We all wanted to go out and play hide-and-go-seek with the neighbor kids and it was after dark and it would be such fun and so on. We were on our way out, not expecting a negative answer, but we were stopped short, much to our surprise.

Much later, years later probably, I understood why. I had come in to her one day and asked her what a particular "word" meant. Anytime you wondered about a word you could ask Hash because that was her forte. All my life I asked her what certain words meant; that is when I miss her so much now, when I hear a new word and wonder about it.

But I knew there was a special significance to "this word" when she quit what she was doing and sat down with me on her lap and asked me where I heard the word. It was from the neighbor boy. She explained that I wasn't old enough to understand it and that she would tell me what it meant when I was old enough. She was very gentle and discrete, but do you know—she never did explain any of that to me even when I did get old enough to understand! She was so glib and talkative about every other subject, but the subject of sex was never easy for her to discuss with us, was it? In fact, it must have been downright impossible, because we never ever had any of those mother and daughter discussions you hear about on TV! I don't know about the rest of you—perhaps you did.

But I've always been proud of the fact that she refused us that game of hide-and-go-seek after dark.

In the spring, roses bloomed in profusion on the rock wall out front, plums hung from the tree by the kitchen window and the old neglected orchard strained to make a showing. During this time, Hash read.

With June came our "release" from school, shooting us like stones from a slingshot headlong into the joys of summer.

Lowell would make a beeline for the pond and we would climb the white sycamore trees beside it like monkeys; we would roam the woody fields, searching for adventure with a capital A. Often we found it. Once it was in the form of robbing a honey tree. Once it was being caught up in a tree when a mean bull snorted below us. (Actually it was probably only a "big cow".) Once it was men up on a hill shooting at us with real guns! They turned out to be hunters, shooting at rabbits in the other direction. But back then we were young and fearless and with Lowell to lead us there. was bound to be danger and excitement right over the next hill. We were ready for it and we went seeking it.

As we played, Hash worked at the "jobs of summer". She cooked for the "work-hands" that Daddy hired to work in the tobacco crop. She really enjoyed cooking big meals and I feel like her when I cook for the men that help Gadie in the summer: Harlan Rutledge, Tom Gordley, Brian Smith, Roy Rutledge, Don Dawson, Randy Patten, Jeff Traylor, etc.

I remember her saying, "I love to cook for the work-hands just as long as I have plenty to cook". She would come out of the kitchen carrying big bowls of vegetables and fried chicken and her famous rolls and set them on the dining room table with a look of pride on her face.

I can remember waking to the sound of the old hens clucking under my window and feeling the sun in my eyes. It made me happy. Then I would get up and run pell-mell down the hill to the pond with a cup in my hand to fill with blackberries. Then back to the house to pour cream and sugar over them for my breakfast. Life was simple and for me, very good.

Through all this, Hash would be taking advantage of the garden bounty, canning the summer and bottling the sunshine for the winter ahead. I didn't appreciate it very much then; I hardly ever remember helping. But now when I do the same work I can feel her sense of satisfaction with each jar I can. I have often said the little sound the jars make as they are sealing, one at a time, is the nicest little sound I can imagine.

When fall came we were as busy as squirrels, gathering walnuts to sell. This was all under Lowell's' supervision, as supervisors didn't have to work very much, as well as I remember, even though all the rest of us were scurrying here and there to gather the walnuts. I believe we used a little wagon, and Hash was reading.

Then the walnuts were spread on the road in front of our house to let the cars run over them to hull them. Can't you just smell them now?

The old pear tree hung heavy with its golden ripe fruit and the pawpaws and wild grapes were there for the picking. While we did these things, Hash read.

The winters were not too special; I don't remember much about them. We had the grate going and we sat around as close to it as we could get.

When we first moved "up on the hill", and when we children were still quite young, I can remember all five of us running to the bed where Hash and Daddy were sleeping and pouncing headlong on them in the morning, thus precipitating a rough and tumble free-for-all. That's a fun memory.

Hash made a lot of biscuits and gravy. And winter was such a marvelous time to curl up and read!

But then, one day, we were growing up. It was not sudden and quick; it didn't happen overnight. It seems, in retrospect, that our childhood stretched out forever.

Now, life became more upbeat and modern. I was a teenager; that changes not only your own life but others around you as well.

Lowell, you decided to go off to see the world, via the Navy. That, in effect, broke up our nest. It was sad, seeing you leave....

But you wrote letters regularly and came home on leaves (and often between leaves) and you did see the world. Judging from the wide variety of girl's pictures you sent home and the anecdotes that accompanied them, a large portion of the female population abroad saw you too!

Once Hash and Daddy took you back to the ship in Norfolk and they were so pleased to get to go on board and inspect the entire ship.

I was the proud recipient of a "status shirt"—one of your "summer whites", the white Navy shirt with sailor collar. How proud I was with that—I was fifteen years old.

You looked so "spiffy" with a Navy uniform on; once I heard you say a sailor could walk down the street with it on and get any girl around.

We would keep up with the Seventh Fleet and it's location and then we would hear on the news that it was being sent here and there, to wherever trouble spots were, I suppose. I was always so proud to say that you were in the Seventh Fleet.

Then Hash did the most uncharacteristic thing imaginable; she "struck out" and got herself a job!

I have been presenting this from my viewpoint and telling how carefree and happy I was and indeed I was. But I didn't have to be concerned with the daily cares of food and money and clothing, etc. Hash was a person who "made do" with little; she had no aspirations whatsoever for anything "grand". But at that time in our life she felt the need for a little something more.

When we were given clothes by friends or when Sheila made us pretty dresses, Hash made sure that the length was right. She once said that it was the most pitiful sight to see a little girl with a long dress on that the mother hadn't cared enough to hem (or lengthen it). I always remembered that. And also, our shoestrings were always clean. She could not tolerate dingy shoestrings—I too felt the same thing when I had babies, and they wore little high-topped shoes. I was fanatical about it, and I always looked at other baby's shoestrings to see how much their mother "cared" for them. I was so proud of Carolyn when I heard that she polished her little Jeff's shoes and changed his shoestrings everyday while he took his nap. Truly she was one of "Holly's Pups".

I dressed baby Tracy in short wool pants and knee socks and white shoes; his coat and hat were pale blue velvet. I thought he would always be "neat and cute". Then, to my amazement, he grew a little and started wanting to wear those ugly tennis shoes! *Only* those ugly tennis shoes— and then and there I lost the battle of the clean white shoestrings!

But even though back then it didn't penetrate my thoughts or cloud my world at all, the fact is that there were no extras in our life.

On the rare occasions when she did have a small "pittance" to spend, she most always spent it on us. One of these occasions might have been the time she opened her cold cream jar one night and found a five dollar bill folded and tucked inside. Bubble had been to visit us that day—need I say more....

Once, a door-to-door salesman came to our house, selling encyclopedias. He made his sales pitch, and couldn't seem to accept Hash's polite refusal of his offer. After listening to his back-up offer several more minutes, where he tried to persuade her to pay by the week, Hash dismissed him with these firm decisive words of wisdom: "You can't get blood out of a turnip".

The simple fact was that even though we had many more needs now as we were growing up and becoming more aware of the world, there was no extra money to fill those needs. Things like that made Hash mad. They made her determined and they made the red spot come out on her forehead.

In front of the drug store that is now Fitch's, but then was Hamilton's, I witnessed a little demonstration of her abject anger and humiliation at not having any money to call her own.

She looked nice, dressed in a black dress or suit and she was fighting mad as she came out of that drug store and started down the street. Lindsay was standing there and I heard her tell him, "I'm just sick and tired of never ever having a nickel to spend". She was so mad she was on the verge of tears and that red spot was glowing! That incident could have triggered her decision to seek a job.

I recall her telling us that she wanted to work so she could buy the little things we needed and wanted, at school for instance, and things that otherwise we could not have, period.

She started working at Georgetown College and no task was too menial for her at the beginning. She cleaned the bathrooms for awhile, then she got a chance to work in the "Grill". She was there for quite a while and seemed to enjoy it. We certainly did enjoy it because she would bring home the most delectable glazed donuts imaginable from there. To us that was a treat too great for words—how we gloried in those donuts!

During that time, as she served the college students, she also closely observed them and she would tell me little things about how some were so popular and how others were silly and what set some apart from others. Just little thumbnail descriptions that gave me things to use as a pattern of things to avoid; they were little points that she shared with me.

Soon she was given a much better job there as she had proven her capability and dependability. It was in a little office in the back of a college dormitory and she had the job of keeping inventory of the storeroom.

We were big enough to stay by ourselves while she worked that summer, and we enjoyed ourselves. Mary Ann, you and I played paperdolls by the hour on that old round kitchen table. We had Dagwood and Blondie, and hundreds of catalog people and Summer Girl and Winter Girl, etc. What fun we had!

Now while she worked, we played Monopoly by the hours. We would have it all spread out on the table and after several hours we would call for a break. Then Mary, you would spring into action and whip up a batch of oatmeal cookies "from scratch" and I would fix Pepsis. It would be ready in a matter of minutes. The next day we would reverse the jobs, I doing the cookies and you the Pepsis, and "the game" would continue. The Pepsis were another of our much appreciated "extras".

One classic story that I will never forget and one which we often re-tell concerns Cokes or the lack of Cokes in our lives. Daddy had given us all a great surprise one night and brought in hotdogs to be cooked. We sat around the table, delighted with our unexpected treat and in the thoughtless way that children often seem to have, one of us piped up and said, "Sure would be nice to have a Coke with this". I almost choke inside with a laughter I can't do justice to when I recall Daddy's completely frustrated, downhearted reply to that unappreciative upstart (probably it was me). He said simply, "Never satisfied".

Another incident regarding "satisfaction" was repeated fairly often around the table; Hash would look at Daddy at the other end of the table after a nondescript meal and say, "You don't look satisfied". I love that, and I often say it to Gadie.

The taste of Coke in little play cups, doll dishes, sticks in my memory too. We would sit in the front yard and have tea parties. I guess that was in your honor, Alice. Remember that picture of you and Mary in the front yard, sipping "tea" over that little barrel table?

Remember the swing in that big tree? I think we used to push you back and forth and much too high in it.

Winter made the "job" much more difficult. Hash would ride home with a neighbor man but when he got to his house he was "not allowed" to drive her the rest of the way home; she had to get out in the snow and zero weather or whatever the occasion and walk the other mile home. A wife's jealousy is never a pleasant thing, is it?

But she perservered and as far as I can remember, she didn't feel sorry for herself one iota. We would watch for her coming through the snow, usually carrying a sack or two, and we'd be ready for her!

I started to say we would see her come "trudging" through the snow, but I changed that, because Hash never ever "trudged". Always she had a spring and a grace to her step—always. And don't you forget it.

While I'm on the subject of "trudging up the hill" I must tell you about the cold wintry night that Daddy and Rube got stuck while trying to drive up that hill. They gave up on trying to drive and decided to walk over a mile home in the zero weather. But they had something to sustain them and spur them on; it was the prospect of hot steaming oyster stew at the end of the journey! They selected the sack containing the oysters and left the other groceries back in the car. The nearer they got to home the more anxious they became for the hot stew. Before they even warmed up or took off their boots, Daddy triumphantly pulled out the oysters for Hash to fix— only the "oysters" was a box of hominy! They had picked up the wrong sack!

So back to Hash, coming in with her sack of groceries—we would have the house all cleaned up, the kitchen work done and the little stove all fired up with coal. After helping her out of her wet clothes and boots we would rub her feet dry, then turn the covers down for her to curl up in the good warm bed.

In minutes we would bring her a plate with her favorite supper on it; bacon and eggs and toast and coffee! Oh, how she bragged on us and how she appreciated it! She would just snuggle up and revel in our attention— she certainly deserved it. I'm sure we didn't follow that routine every night, but Daddy wasn't there much and we were more than glad to fix her supper and "minister" to her after what she had been through all day for us.

Not one time do I remember her ever coming in with a scowl or a sharp word; it was always smiles and happiness at being back home with us. Now, remembering that, I am always at the door when Scarlett and Tracy come in from school; I have never greeted them with anything but smiles and love....

About this time, Elvis came into my life, and Hash accepted him from the start. She loved him too, in her paternal way. She always shared with me the thrill of each new song and each new experience; she never thought I was foolish in my love for him.

One of my greatest satisfactions came when she went with Gadie and me to see him in Cincinnati. I had already been to see him in concert twice and I got to go once more after this particular one, but I could see him through Hash's eyes this time, and that made it even more special. From the moment he exploded on stage in the swirl of his bejeweled white cape until he vanished beyond the frenzied screaming crowd between us, I felt a special satisfaction that we came full circle to sharing this shining moment.

So with her "new money" she was able to put on "lay-away" something that became my most prized possession—a little record player! Not a stereo in a console, not an elaborate sound system, but to me the most unbelievable acquisition imaginable! I was so happy I was delirious when she told me—it didn't matter that it would take weeks and weeks of paying a few dollars out of her slim paycheck before she could bring it home—just the knowledge that it was sitting there with my name on it was excitement enough!

Right then I started buying Elvis' records—for 79¢ apiece—little singles. I would save my money until I had enough to get one, then start again on the next one. Hash laughingly said that I was probably the only girl around who started buying records before I had anything to play them on.

Then one day she brought it home with her and I must have played it constantly without stopping for the next two years at least. It was tan and portable—very small like a suitcase.

I took it to school and Geraldine and Betty and I would rush to the bathroom and listen to a quick stanza of "Don't Be Cruel" between classes; it was like a much needed "fix", a musical "fix".

When I stayed all night with one of them, there it was between us in the bed, under the covers so the parents couldn't hear it all night! How I appreciated her buying it for me! And she knew it too—there was no wondering on her part if I liked it like we parents sometimes do today with gifts.

After the gift of the little record player, it was just a year or so until I almost collided with Elvis himself! He made one of his three appearances on the Ed Sullivan Show and there I was on the same stage—but alas, a week later!

When a woman reaches her forties, she has come to a stepping stone, a crossover, a turning point, but regardless of what the time is called, there is no turning back. However, she may turn her life in any other direction except backwards.

She must decide if the years behind her measured up to what she expects, or indeed desires, the next two score to be.

For this reason there is often a vague uneasiness, an unspoken dissatisfaction in people's feelings at this time of their life. I say "people", because I firmly believe that men also go through this period, and that it is not to be confused with the so called "change of life".

Daddy was the first one to alert me to this transient period of a person's life; in doing so he was attempting to explain what happened to their marriage and to examine the whys and wherefores of a woman's emotions at such a time.

It is to Daddy's eternal credit and an acknowledgment of his intelligence that he could have the insight to see all of this, and to understand the internal workings of a heart and mind.

This is not to say that he didn't put up a heart-rending fight, which was dreadful to watch, using every promise and plea, and every artful wile at his disposal to win her back.

But her mind was made up. She had charted a different course for her remaining years; she had put behind her the disappointments and the deprivations as well as the joys and times of laughter.

After twenty years together, their marriage came to an end in March of 1958, thus bringing to a close the summer of her life.

*AUTUMN:*

"Maturity" was becoming to Hash. As is the case with many women, she seemed to glory in the fullness of her years; she emitted a special aura that comes only with time.

James Jones worked out of the same little office at the college where she worked. She saw him day in and day out, and he adored her.

At first he adored her only from a distance, and dared not to put his love into words.

But as is often the case with people who are thrown together numerous times a day, politeness becomes familiarity; admiration becomes outright adoration and dissatisfaction paves the way for changes.

In Hash's life and beliefs there was no room for immorality; none whatsoever. So even though she married James soon after her divorce and it is common knowledge that he was completely enraptured by her even before then, she is not to be condemned for it.

In view of the morals of people in general today, she was concerned that I should know the truth about her relationship with James in her time of transition. She adamantly assured me that James was "a perfect gentleman" in all aspects of their short courtship before marriage and any who knew her and who knew James could be as positive as me that she was above reproach. Of that I have no doubts whatsoever.

And so they were married—on March 23, 1958. Ironically, their twentieth anniversary fell just at the time when we first knew she was really ill. James set the bottle of champagne they had bought for the occasion back on a shelf, until she felt well enough to enjoy it........and there it sits to this day.

Their life together began in a little red shingled house at the very end of East Main Street.

Hash came into the marriage bringing two little tables, her clothes and personal belongings—and three daughters.

Daddy's only demand had been that you should stay with him, Billy. I often wonder how it must have affected you and when I do, I hurt for you. So young and faced with such a change. As it turned out, you were eventually staying with Kay and Lindsay, not Daddy, therefore you were deprived of both parents, actually. How you must have suffered; I didn't have sense enough to realize it then. You must have resentment; do you curse the fates?

I remember Hash saying that it would be just temporary and until then, she could have you with her on the weekends......it never worked out that way though, did it?

We were in a totally new element "in our new town home." Life was certainly much different and we liked it. We even had a TV! And there were two bedrooms upstairs for we three girls to share.

Mary Ann, you and I were delighted with the chance to be so close to "town." We could even walk if we had to, but there was James going back and forth all the time and we could go anytime we wanted to.

Alice, you were small, just about nine, and I can remember your little "pixie haircut." You were in a sort of limbo, reacting to the change, as we all were.

I always picture you playing around outside the yard fence, in that little field across the road. I don't know what you were playing—you were just over there a lot.

Now we own the twenty acres directly across from the little red house. I ride through that field sometimes with Gadie and I look over there and remember......sometimes I tell him he should buy the little house and move it across the road. Like a little shrine, you know. (I am making a joke. Whatever else you do, don't take me seriously on everything I say—or write.)

In the interval after her divorce and before her remarriage, Hash lived in the Georgetown Hotel, so as to be close to her job. Mary Ann, Alice and I divided our time between her, Momma and Bubble and Daddy.

At the time we were "home" with Daddy, there was naturally a lot of tension, considering the situation and the strain he was undergoing.

At times he would lash out with angry words at something I had done (or more likely at something I *hadn't* done but should have) and it would hurt my feelings. I would go off by myself, resolving never to forgive him, and then a little later, here he would come, doing what he always did ever since I can remember: He would put that big long arm around my shoulders and half hug and half choke me and say "You my buddy?" And then I couldn't keep from laughing and he would keep asking me over and over until I finally said "yes." It was absolutely frustrating to try to be mad, and to enjoy being mad, and to know that he wouldn't allow it.

Wasn't that a fine way to dispel resentment and brooding? In retrospect I see the wisdom in that approach, and indeed I use it with Scarlett and Tracy.

Also, at this period of time, Mary Ann and I stayed at Aunt Ann's and Uncle Joe's some. Mommau was staying there too, and it was good to be with her. When I think of Mommau, I see her as being fine boned and almost transparent with her smooth white hair pulled back in a twist. She didn't wear a little "knot" like Momma; it seems like she usually had a "french twist."

Miss Mary and Miss Fannie. How strange that sounds. Our two grandmothers, both in their 80's and how blessed we were to have them. But it was not to be for long.

Speaking of Mommau's "french twist" reminds me of when we lived with her and how she would fix my hair every morning. She would bring a pan of water and set it beside her rocking chair with me on the floor between her knees. After wetting me down good, she would part my hair in the middle and then plait it so tight I could barely stand it. But the real trouble started when it began to dry. It would tighten up, raising my eyebrows and ears several inches in the process! By noon I couldn't even blink my eyes!

When I would stay all night with Momma, before sending me off to school she would administer a face scrubing that completely belied her gentle nature. Using red Lifebuoy soap, she would grasp me by the neck and as I gritted my teeth and squeezed my eyes shut, she would really scrub me down good.

But it would be forgotten by the time I sat down at the table because I got something there that was a very special treat—coffee! It was a regular routine for Momma to pour coffee for everyone at the table and the fact that you were a child didn't exclude you. I can still see her sloshing the cream into my cup before pouring the coffee; sometimes now I do that and I am her.

During this period of time, my most glorious moment occurred: I met Gaylord, better known as Gadie! It was a moment that was to change and shape my life, to set my course for the future, and to culminate in a lifetime together.

We were introduced by Shirley and Kenny, we talked for a few brief moments and then we went our separate ways. That might have been it except for a flat tire sometime later.

Daddy was taking Mary and me back to town after a visit with him and he stopped to give a lift to two men who had a flat tire in the country. It was Gadie and his brother Bud!

Gadie had on a white goatskin jacket and when he waved goodbye to us, Mary Ann, remember how we talked about his white teeth flashing?

Later, over the phone we discovered that we both misunderstood the others name; I thought he was Eddie, he thought I was Tammy.

The song "Tammy" being popular then had no doubt contributed to his mistaking my name for that. He said all week he had been thinking of me as "Tammy."

Therefore I, not knowing that I would be with him from then on, said that he could just call me that. So he did, and so he still does, but I never ever think of myself as anything but "Fannee." Never.

Mommau had leukemia and she grew progressively weaker. That is the only symptom I can remember—the weakness. She wasn't bedfast or in pain, but she had to go to the hospital at regular intervals for transfusions.

Then came the time when she told Kay and Aunt Ann and Daddy that she didn't want to keep on with the transfusions......She was old and frail and they were too taxing on her........and quietly they accepted her decison. It was hers to make.

I was sitting in a swing with her at Aunt Ann's porch, long before Gadie and I were married or even said we planned to marry and she called me "Mrs. Hilander"........She seemed quite pleased by her witty intuition and especially when I smilingly acknowledged it.

And so she died on August 8, 1958 at eighty-six years of age.

Hash worked at a restaurant in town as a waitress; James got a job at the Veteran's Hospital.

I was dating Gadie regularly now and Hash liked him. She liked him because I did; she usually respected my decisions.

Once Gadie wore long underwear under his pants and deliberately let them hang out an inch or two. Having told Mary Ann and me ahead of time, he pretended not to know it, so as to see Hash's reaction.

She was highly indignant when she saw us giggling and looking at them and she tried to get us to be quiet so we wouldn't embarrass him.

Somewhere along that time he started calling her "Big Greasy Momma," and she always got such a kick out of that title.

A few years before she died she made the remark that it made no difference to her what anyone had to say about Gadie, one way or the other; to her he was perfect because, she said, in all these years "Fannee has never had one bad word to say about him and that's what counts." I appreciated that comment—and that loyalty.

June 11, 1959 was the day Gadie and I married—two weeks after I graduated from school.

It was strange that at the time I evidently had not one vestige of sentimentality concerning the day; stranger still considering the fact I am on a never-ending sentimental journey now.

So she and I took the event in stride and accepted it as just another wedding day. She knew that Daddy had mentioned that he would like to go along, so she very graciously and truthfully said that she didn't mind at all not going. We had a small ceremony in front of a Judge in an office with Sonny Noel and Mary Ann standing up with us, and Daddy was there to make sure the knot was tied right. I'm assuming that it was because it hasn't even started to unravel yet.

I have neither met nor heard of anyone who is more giving or who has more concern for people than Gadie has. He truly "cares," and that outstanding quality of his has earned my respect and admiration. Added to this is the fact that he is the most diligent, concerned father imaginable, constantly considering Scarlett and Tracy's future as well as their present welfare. I love him dearly.

And he loves me. I gave him a little plaque once that sums it all up. It says "Blessed is the man with a wife who loves him as he is and children who respect him as a father."

I marrried in June and then on September 3, 1959 little Momma died. Momma with the dancing black eyes, Momma who crooked her finger over her nose and laughed at you was gone at eighty-two.

She had never been in the hospital until a few days before she died. When Bubble called to say that they had taken Momma to the hospital, I was overcome with a forboding sadness, despite everyone's assurance that a hospital stay was not all that serious.

Nevertheless I sat on the steps outside in the dark and sobbed uncontrollably, fearing the outcome. Indeed she died a few days later.

Soon before she died, maybe the day before, she had me lean over so I could hear her small weak voice. She had something to tell me. I made out the words she uttered, and I repeated it back to her to make sure I had it right. The words were: "I hear my mother calling me like she did when I was a little girl."

That is so close to my heart that I have never been able to even repeat it to more than one or two people.

Hash never talked to me about her sense of loss or sadness after Momma died. I wonder how she felt; I wonder how it affected her.

In the three months between my marriage and Momma's death, something highly important happened to Hash; she embarked upon a path that led her to become one of Jehovah's Witnesses.

In doing so, she at last knew happiness and fulfillment; she truly found her "place in the sun."

For months she and James had set aside a time for Bible reading together and during that time she had sensed that she had no real understanding of what they read. Therefore she prayed that she would gain an understanding and shortly thereafter she did.

In answer to her sincere prayer, she soon gained true insight and knowledge and the Bible opened up before her in all its awesome glory. This grand privilege can be anyone's who truly has a desire to learn; the priceless treasure is there for all who seek for it.

And now her life, which I feel was never clearly defined before, had a grand purpose and she was in perfect control of her life course. She knew where she was going—and she knew how to get there.

One of Jehovah's Witnesses named Ruth had seen fit to come to her house and offer her a home Bible study. The offer was readily and willingly accepted; after all, isn't this what she had prayed for? You might even say opportunity knocked.

In searching the scriptures and having the knowledge unfold before her enlightened eyes, she was returning to "the days of her youth."

Her Poppa had been one of the first Witnesses of Jehovah in the country even before they were called such. Many people had told me of how he would sit "cross-legged" on top of the counter in his store and "witness" to all who came in.

He gloried in discussing the Bible with friend and foe alike; many a thunderous debate sounded through his store. He "knew the truth" and he made sure that others heard it too—at least once.

He was the "character" of the country, the practical joker of renown, the softhearted proprietor and he was bigger than life.

Such a man relates to people—grown people—but seldom to children. Other than the fact that he gathered all the grandchildren together at least once a year and regaled us with the grisly story of "Scabby Headed Jack," we were more or less uninvolved personally with Poppa. At least that is the memory I have; perhaps yours is different.

Nevertheless, the fact that I was singled out one day and talked to very seriously was impressed more deeply upon me in contrast to the previous lack of personal interest.

I stayed with Momma and Poppa a lot and I remember it well. We would all three sit in one room and listen to the stories on the radio. They were a prelude to the soap operas on TV today.

Momma was fascinated by "Stella Dallas" and she would sit with her finger crooked over her nose, listening so intently that you dared not say a word to her. She would lean close to the radio and because she seemed to be staring into it, I always assumed that she was seeing those characters inside of it as they talked.

After her stories were over Poppa's favorite came on—"Lorenzo Jones!"

Now Momma hated that story and when Poppa wasn't looking she would make a "yucky" face at me. Then she and I would slip into the kitchen in the dark and she would pull a big cake pan from under a table and cut me a slice of the most delectable black fruit cake that a human ever tasted! That was our special treat.

In the course of an evening, while sitting before the grate and doing whatever the moment entailed, occasionally a great resounding "burp" would echo through the room.

Startled, I would look from one to the other, expecting a shamefaced "excuse me" from whomever emitted that sound but no such apology was forthcoming. In fact, no attention was even paid to the occurrence and I gradually realized that when two people grow old together, such things as that and seeing one another with their false teeth removed was acceptable and normal. Nevertheless, I silently resolved back then as I sat between the two of them that if I ever grew up and married that I would die before I ever let my husband hear me do such a thing. (Where did I go wrong?)

Now back to the subject of Poppa's personal attention to me on one special occasion. There was a little grate in the main room where Poppa always put his big black high-topped shoes and socks every night after he took them off. I can see them sitting there, so full of character, and for some reason they tied in with this other thing I remember.

On the back side of the same wall there was another little grate in his bedroom. For some reason I remember Glenne being connected with that day.

I must have been about five years old because it was sometime before the store burned. Poppa called me in there, singled me out all by myself, and to my amazement he presented me with a little book that was published by the Watchtower Bible and Tract Society. It was titled, "This Means Everlasting Life." Looking at me intently, willing me to understand the importance of what he had to say, he told me, "Now this won't mean anything to you now, but someday it will."

Thank you, Poppa. Someday, which is now, it does mean something to me; it means the world to me. Not the book, but what the book stood for and what it led me to over the years. It led me to a life filled with real purpose and happiness which is what being one of Jehovah's Witnesses means.

To symbolize her dedication to Jehovah God, she was baptized on October 23, 1960. To her great happiness, Mary Ann and I were baptized at the same time as she was.

Now, for the first time in many years, Hash was in her element and she bloomed and matured in the company of the new friends she now had, and her new way of life. The friends she made were friends indeed and remained so until the end. Never once was she let down or disappointed by any of them. I wish I could list all your names but you know who you are and you know she loved you. That will suffice.

Before, she had lived with a certain insecurity and was unable to branch out in any direction; now she regained her confidence and became, in effect, a total woman.

Always intelligent, she now increased her intake of knowledge and polished it to a higher degree. She was able to hold her own in any conversation and indeed to dominate it if she so desired.

Her sense of fashion was heightened and she was able to indulge it somewhat. Having a flair for fashion, she always looked "nice." The cock of her hat, the flash of an eye—they all added up to an attractive woman.

Once she achieved the hair-cut that was flattering to her she stuck with it and was pleased with it. I remember her exclaiming, "I never imagined that my hair could have such a nice shape to it!"

Often when she would come out of the house and get into the car with me, I would marvel at how beautiful she looked. So vibrant and colorful. And I would make sure I told her. There's not much use in looking good if no one tells you, is there? I would say, "You look so pretty I just wish I had a camera." Often I had one and I have gotten some great pictures of her. Pictures are wonderful things to have.

She would have a fur collar up around her face and always have pretty earrings on. She took great care with her make-up and as Tracy said, "She always smelled so good."

The ability to articulate slowly and coherently was never her style, especially when she was enthusiastic about a subject. Most always she was enthusiastic about her subject.

Can't we all just see her now, talking with her hands as well as with her mouth and her eyes flashing or snapping as the occasion demanded.

Words tumbling out, skipping from one subject to another—how those of us who loved her laughed at that "pell-mell" quality of hers.

But, with much concentrated effort on her part, she had gradually taught herself to stick to a subject and follow through on a theme—usually.

She worked as a waitress for several years at two local restaurants, then a better job was procured at the Soil Conservation Office—testing soil. I used to run upstairs at the Post Office to see her and marvel at her adeptness with the little vials of dirt, which seemed complicated to me, but she dismissed it with her customary manner, saying it was "simple." Remember when she called certain people "simpletons?" Couldn't she make that word ring?

Every summer, for the last eighteen years of her life, we traveled to a Watchtower Convention or "assembly." They were held in different cities and by this means she got to see quite a bit of the country and traveled to places where she otherwise would not have been.

What experiences we had together! How we laughed and laughed as we remembered the things that happened.

We always went together and stayed in the same hotel or motel room. We traveled by train, bus or car.

Now assemblies are so dreadfully sad for me—they are probably the hardest time of the year for me because she was always there.

We would go into our hotel after the sessions, dead tired from so much walking, and walk primly through the lobby and up the elevator. Then, after rounding a corner out of sight of other people, she and Scarlett would tear off down the hall at full speed, kicking their shoes off as they ran. It was a ritual, started when Scarlett was only three or four years old and it included Tracy when he learned to walk—and run.

Now, at the hotels, we just walk to our room, but we remember........ and we smile.

She used to love to tell people the story of how she looked down from the twelfth story of a hotel room in Chicago or Milwaukee or Charlottsville, I'm not sure where, and watched Scarlett and me at the swimming pool. She said I was lying in the sun like a cat (she always said I looked and acted like a cat—she used to call me "puss in boots"). When she saw Scarlett's head go under water, she said she was horrified but could only watch helplessly, from so far away. Then she said that I reached out, without ever changing my position, and pulled her in with one hand like an old cat pulling in a little wet kitten. Of course, we were in the shallow water, and probably she was only four stories up. But stories do become embellished as time goes by, don't they?

Another time, we rushed to catch a bus that was literally packed and Scarlett and I were swept onto the bus by the surging crowd, in the back door yet! As the bus pulled away, my frantic eyes caught a glimpse of Hash standing forlornly on the curb; there had been no more room for even one more. Only those of us who know her well can picture the confused, angry look I saw on her face. We laughed uproarously and hilariously after I somehow managed to get the bus stopped and little Scarlett and I were unceremoniously ejected from the back.

Then another time involved Scarlett being kidnapped by an elevator and my wild race to catch the elevator. I had been flipping her in front of me at each elevator door and she would scurry through the door before they closed. She got so adept at it that at one stop she got in and I didn't. I thought she would panic, so I clattered off in my high heels to find the exit to the stairs so I could be at the next floor by the time she was. I jerked the exit door open and ran headlong through it. Only it wasn't an exit—it was a broom closet!

In Nashville, we all went to the Grand Ole Opry together and I remember how well she liked little Marty Robbins. Mary Ann, you and Nelson were just going together then and when we saw you two coming in, she commented that Nelson already had you trained, because you were walking several paces behind him.

Canada really tested her self-control; her endurance was fully put to the test. The fact that the waitresses couldn't understand our language well made ordering an ordeal; the fact that most of their signs and directions were not in our language made transportation a game of guess work.

But she made the best of it, even the subways which we converged upon each morning with fresh determination, defying defeat. The subways were advanced and complicated to us—we barely managed to arrive at our destination and back to our hotel at night. But she kept a stiff upper lip as she descended each morning to the "subway to hell" as she described it.

One evening we were nearing our hotel, by means of the bus, but the driver kept going about three more blocks after we rang to get off. Now when you are tired and feel unable to walk even a few feet, an extra three blocks are hard to overlook. As I stepped down out of the bus, I was aware that Hash had stopped in front of the hapless driver and was glaring at him with her hands on her hips. Mustering up all the self-control and dignity she had within her I heard her say, "All I've got to say is that if I ever get out of this awful place and get back home to Kentucky, I'll never leave again as long as I live!"

Indeed she was a "sight"—a unique woman who was a friend to most all she knew. She was fun to be around; she brightened up a room with her funny ways.

I thought I knew her well and I thought I understood her; now I'm not so sure I knew anything except what she wanted me to know.

In all sincerity I remarked to you, Mary Ann, that I thought Hash was a perfectly happy, contented woman. To my astonishment you disagreed completely with me when you said, "Oh no, she was miserable most of the time."

Who is to say which observation was the correct one? I saw reflected in her what I felt and what I looked for; you in turn saw what you expected her to be.

The last place she lived was the little green house that she and James moved into on Etta Lane. She loved it there and seemed perfectly content—she and James and Gi-Gi. Gi-Gi, the fat white poodle dog. I never liked Gi-Gi. Hash told me I should at least speak to her when I came in so I wouldn't hurt her feelings.

She and James took her with them everywhere just like a child. They would order a hamburger or Colonel Sanders chicken for her when they ordered for themselves. Can you imagine? Hash with a poodle dog that thought it was a child, and our Daddy with a CAT!!

Remember when we were all at home and if an unfortunate cat should be so brave as to venture in front of Daddy, he would sent it sailing through the air—with his foot. He despised our family cats—Moon and Twinkle Toes and Tiger, etc.

That reminds me of the enormous black and white Tom cat that obliged us with his presence periodically, when he needed a rest from his mysterious dark wanderings, here and there. Hash would be making biscuits and he would stand and beg until she would pitch him pieces of the raw dough. She liked old Tom.

I don't remember whether he made any impression on Daddy or not, but I would say he didn't, considering Daddy's intense dislike for the feline family. But now as you all know, that Siamese cat named "Dixie" has made a complete fool of Daddy.

Oh, the way we change—people and their pets—a book in itself.

So sure of Gi-Gi's intelligence was Hash that she got to the point where she would spell BATH, otherwise she insisted that if Gi-Gi heard the vulgar word she would retreat under the couch and could not be retrieved.

I'm glad James still has her; it will be terrible when something happens to her. Hash used to say that she didn't think she could stand it if anything happened to Gi-Gi.

They were a familiar sight taking their daily walks along Etta Lane. Hash laughingly said that on their walks she would start down Hazelwood and Gi-Gi would head toward Dogwood Drive.

How lonely James must be, losing his wife, his mother and his brother in barely more than a year.

James had a greenhouse and a large garden and he and Hash set up a fruitstand right out of town. It was a lovely sight to me with the baskets of golden corn and green beans and luscious tomatoes piled high, but my enthusiasm was not shared by Hash. This was clearly not "her cup of tea," and I laugh when I remember a picture I saw of her, perched in the opening at the front of the building. On her face was surely the most distressed, bored expression I had ever seen and it was so pitiful, it was funny. It even made her laugh to see it.

She spent her last years in a way that made her happy; I have no regrets for her lifestyle.

Being a "Witness" made her life content as nothing else ever could. Never missing meetings, she was an encouragement to all and she found great satisfaction in "going out in service." I recall her telling me, "When I wake up in the morning and know that I'm going out in service, I just feel so happy." How wonderful!

She found delight in her Bible studies with her special friends—Katherine, Edith, Mrs. Snelling, Margaret, Francis and many others over the years that I don't even remember. In fact, her friend Edith was the very first visitor at the funeral home, sitting there with such a look of quiet sadness. Unbelieving, as we all were.

She kept little Shane a couple of days a week; he was her special guest. Once I heard her say, "It's never imposing on me at all to keep Shane. He has never been here except as my invited guest." He had some of his toys there; he rode his "Boom-Boom" through the house. A long time after she died, I would still see his little trucks and cars out in the front yard as I drove by.

She laughed, she played, she worked. Sir Pizza and the Pondorosa Steak House were the places she and James frequented. She hated Saturdays; she was bored and restless then. It was like a plague to her. On Sundays she usually cooked lunch for Alice and Shane and herself. Chicken and noodles, rolls, etc.

Shelia would come down a day or two a week from Lexington and take Hash and Bubble shopping and to lunch. Just like they used to do, years ago. That was good.

And through it all, she read. And she read. Curled up on the couch, with her feet tucked under her—content. The public library and the Watchtower Society were her constant sources of material—her lifeline and her enjoyment.

When Alice and I packed her little bag to take to the hospital on the final trip we tucked her little paper-back novel and her sweet worn Bible in but needless to say, she was completely oblivious to them, for the first time........and the last.

Now the autumn of her life was slowly coming to an end, unbeknownst to us, and in all probability, to her.

As late as December, just four months before she died, she was still the perfect, vibrant Hash we had always had—the same one we always expected to have.

But now, "the days dwindled down to a precious few" and then she was no more.........

*WINTER*:

There was no winter.

# 4
# THE WINTER
# OF HER DISCONTENT

For a woman who all her life had a love affair with books and a passion for words I consider it fitting to present the account of her final days in the form of a conclusion to a fine book.

She ended the chapters of her life the same way she lived them, uncomplainingly and without demands, causing as little commotion as possible.

In fact, her desire for calmness was obsessive. I can remember her always talking about how wonderful it was to remain calm and to lead a calm life. One of her favorite scriptures was about the importance of a calm heart and I've heard her quote that numerous times. Also, she would tell me at times she would be thankful in her prayers for a calm peaceful day or night. That meant a lot to her.

I'm not saying she always remained calm because she didn't. She could get heated up and agitated at people and situations and we have all seen her at those times. Remember that red spot below her widow's peak—watch out when that turned red! That meant she was mad or insulted or more likely that someone had hurt her feelings, since she was a highly sensitive person. Very highly sensitive.

There are so many incidents in my memory of when she got her feelings hurt because of her sensitivity. Not that she took offense easily, just that she took a lot of things personally. Mary Ann, I believe you're like her in that regard. Aren't you?

I wish I could slap everyone who ever hurt her feelings on purpose. Once I shook my fist at someone I shouldn't have because they had been unkind to her. That tickled her and when she mentioned it over the years we always laughed.

The winter of 77-78 was dreadful, equaled only somewhat by the preceding winter. We were all snowed in for weeks and schools were closed for six weeks and life came to a virtual standstill for many of us. That, to me, was a joy and I reveled in it. Being snowbound is what I consider happiness, but it is tinged with guilt feelings when I consider what hardships it puts upon many people.

Anyway, I think Hash enjoyed it for awhile, but that soon it became overpowering to her. She had plenty of good food and a warm house all winter and for that we can be thankful.

Now, she who was used to going all the time was unable to go and it bothered her after a time. Going to meetings and "going out in service" was her life and now she could do neither.

On days that others got out and would have taken her too, she had an odd reluctance to venture out on the slick spots. She said she was so afraid she would fall and break a bone, and that was totally out of character for her. The winter before she would sally past me on the ice as I picked my way carefully along, fearing a fall. She told me that was the only way not to fall, just to loosen up and not fear it and indeed it worked for her because she never slipped.

In fact, she really prided herself on her agility which never before failed her. When she was almost sixty-two she went to a skating party, donned a pair of skates and sailed away on them, even though she hadn't been on skates since she was a child! Her days when she was a youngster in Lexington were filled with many happy hours of roller-skating down the side-walk and as she said, once you learn you never forget, just like bike riding.

She really enjoyed skating at that party—she said she felt exhilarated—as light as a feather.

The doctor in Lexington when she had her radiation treatments had told her that it took most of the calcium out of her bones and she realized that a broken bone would be a real problem to heal properly if indeed it would heal at all. So one day shortly after the skating party she said to me, "You know, I just realized what a foolish unnecessary risk I would be taking by skating like that if I fall. I got it out of my system by knowing I could still do it, so I'm not going to try that anymore."

We all remember her reputation of being able to put her leg over her head and around her neck. How proud she was of that and of all the extreme twists and turns she could do without ever getting tired or sore.

She had the greatest admiration for agility; she never wanted to lose it. I'm glad she never had to get old and stiff. Some people say she couldn't have accepted old age. We'll never know, and I feel a small measure of satisfaction that she never had to accept it; who could picture her as a little old woman?

Hash would have been proud of Uncle Pal at the reunion last year when he jumped up on our trampoline and without practicing turned a perfect flip! Of course, she would have been impelled to outdo him........

When we had the horses named Jubilee and Baldy, she said she admired people who could swing effortlessly up into the saddle, so of course she wanted to see if she could do it. I saddled one of them up, she swung into the saddle (on the second try) and then, she was satisfied. No, she didn't want to ride, and she immediately dismounted after her successful mounting of the mount.

Once she had one or two of us on a bike with her and she hadn't ridden one for years, but we sailed down that Sam Williamson hill with the greatest of ease, just like we were air-borne.

So she stayed in and she worried—something she did very little of before. All her life she seemed to escape the worrying that most people do—or at least she concealed it well. I personally think she didn't worry—she really applied her theory that things would turn out alright.

Maybe she could tell now that things would not turn out alright—not this winter—so she worried.

She worried out loud about some things, but there must have been a lot of the worry that was repressed.

It's alright to repress emotions for awhile. But it's a wonderful thing to pull them out at the end of the day when you are alone or with someone who cares. Then you should cry over what you couldn't cry over earlier; then you should get angry over what you repressed earlier; then you should laugh loud and long at what you were not allowed to laugh over at the time. But what are you to do with the worry—where is it to go—how can it be dispelled? I must ask Dr. Stoll about that at our next session........

How ironic that she who always told Bubble not to worry about getting sick because she, being ten years younger and in good health would always be there to take care of her, should go first. She truly delighted in Bubble's company and enjoyed their relationship thoroughly. How nice that they could be so close in the last years—visiting and shopping and talking on the phone each day. Shelia and the two of them would go out a time or two each week and eat at nice places and shop and just be together. Lowell, you told me how much you appreciated Shelia doing that for her and I do too. She got to do a lot more that way and she enjoyed it. She always loved "little Shelia," as she called her.

So she worried about not getting to the meetings, but the worst part, as she told me, was the indecision of whether or not she should try to go. That shows that she was not herself and that the illness inside of her was manifesting itself. She said, "I just can't stand the indecision of whether or not to go and it just tears me up. Once I decide one way or the other I am alright." She, who never worried, did so now and I failed to see the connection and to heed the warning signs.

Bubble told me that she said, "I'm tired of not seeing Fannee except to turn around at the meeting and see her for a minute."

I didn't have enough sense to see the signals and the trouble signs—I too had adopted her habit of not worrying. I go through life in a haze and I see what I want to see, I suppose. I did not want to see that my mother was changing so I honestly did not see it.

But Bubble, with her intense intuition, did see trouble. However, when she exposed her fears to me, they were by then in the past-tense where all good fears belong. She said, "I've been real worried about Hazel. She hasn't been herself at all for awhile." That took me by surprise and I quickly explained it away: "Why, it's been such a bad winter and she has been in so long. She has cabin fever." Cabin fever can cover a multitude of sins—but not illnesses. Bubble was right in her perceptiveness. And I was not that sharp.

But she said in the same conversation that Hash had started sounding like herself again and she was relieved that she was getting back to normal. She told me about James taking Hash and her to Lexington—the roads being decent again—and how Hash wanted to go in one of the stores but only for a few minutes. She stressed that point of not wanting to stay but a very few minutes—she who was always ready to go and shop around—and wanting to get back home soon. The item she bought was significant—a robe.

Bubble also noticed that she was always anxious to get home and get her clothes off and into a robe. We didn't realize it, but any pressure on her must have been highly uncomfortable. Did she know why?

James braved the elements one night to take her to one of the steak houses in Lexington because she had a desire to "get out." It was obvious then that she wasn't feeling well and had no appetite, so the idea of the steak and baked potato appealed to her somewhat. To me it is so sad because she wanted so badly to be back to normal, but when she got her plate she could eat no more than one bite of potato.

Following my conversation with Bubble about cabin fever, I called Alice and suggested that the four of us get out for lunch and a movie. We all needed a lift and what better way than that? The plans were laid and away we went—carefully—through the snow which was still with us but much less so.

Our lunch was delightful and brings fond memories each time I remember it. We ate at a Japanese place because Hash always liked oriental food.

This day we all ordered something different so we could share—chop suey—chow mein—spring chicken. It was served in large silver covered bowls and hot tea came in a pretty pot. We all ate excessively, passing the silver bowls back and forth and pouring more tea.

There was much joking and laughing and bowing to the little waiter. We always had fun together. Hash was a fun person always, looking for and finding the humor in life—and this day was just one of many.

Next, we ventured forth to the nearby movie which I had selected because it seemed to be just what we needed to see.

Being a Sophia Loren movie called "One Special Day," I naturally assumed it would be a thrilling love story and I informed the others that she would be wearing lovely clothes and what a treat we were in for and so on.

To make a long story short it was in black and white, with subtitles for those of us who couldn't speak Italian, with the entire wardrobe of Miss

Loren consisting of one extremely dowdy housedress worn throughout the film as she tried to strike up a romance with a man who finally confessed he was a homosexual!

How we laughed then and later at my ability to "pick a loser," but regardless of that, "our last day out" with Hash was a complete success, wasn't it Alice?

That incident reminded me of the time several years ago when we went to see the "Graduate" together and how shocked she was. Surprisingly enough, considering how razor sharp she was about everything else, sexual insinuations usually went way above her head. She never grasped the fact about the homosexual in the above mentioned movie, even though it was obvious to the rest of us—even to Bubble. I'm glad she was a "babe as to badness" in many ways.

So with the break in the extreme weather, we were encouraged and anxious to get back to our regular routines; we were all unaware of the subtle changes taking place in Hash. Hastening to a close was the winter of '77; it was leaving with more than we would know.

# 5
# DID SHE KNOW?

Losing a mother is most surely the hardest thing one has to endure in life, in my opinion. I know others will have differing thoughts and of course it depends on the closeness of the relationship and other factors.

The ultimate security is having a mother of your very own—losing her deprives you of more than words can say.

The question foremost in my mind for a long time and still pondered is—did she know?

When a person gradually loses the health and vitality which she was blessed with profusely for so many years and feels pain and weakness come upon her, she naturally knows something is very wrong. I just wonder if she really knew what terribly bad things were happening in her body or if like us she thought it was a massive infection. I held to that assumption to the very end—refusing to think otherwise and I was more or less backed up by the doctor in that thought.

But so many things make me think she did know and was just shielding us from the knowledge. At other times I think just the opposite— that she too believed it was a temporary problem which would clear up.

If she did know, why did she feel she had to shield and protect us from such things? We could have handled it, couldn't we? But she was always like that and since she seemed invincible we grew to think of her that way.

If she knew, I wish I could have shared her fears and questions. A person shouldn't have to handle that all alone.

Putting these events in the order they happened, I will relate the reasons why I feel like maybe she did know what was happening.

When we first realized she was ill in some way, I would go up each day to check on her. I wouldn't knock, and she would always be on the couch, usually sitting cross-legged. I remember she would have a different look on her face, as if she had been sitting there for hours contemplating unspoken thoughts. I felt like she was worried and wanted to tell me more, but I never got any more than the usual answers from her when I would anxiously ask her how she was. She hadn't been reading and the TV was never on—it was just her sitting there upright with a robe on-thinking.

Lillian Williams, her soul-mate for many, many years, stayed with her for about an hour on one of her last days at home. She had been through more pain than we knew or suspected and she told Lillian that if it wasn't for all the sadness it would put us through she would much rather just go on and die. But it was evidently no more than two weeks that this pain was so bad because only then did she really let us know she was sick.

The next reason I have is the last doctor's visit we made. This visit was with Dr. F., a specialist in such problems, and as soon as he examined her he went to phone for a hospital room. She leaned her head weakly over on the table and said—much more to herself than to me—"James can just go live with his mother." My mind absolutely refused to take any note of the significance of that until much later.

Before that, so cleverly concealed was the pain and such a front was put up that we didn't conceive of such a thing as her being really sick. Once we did, she was given some pain pills to help her along and these kept her in a sleepy limbo and only occasionally did she reveal the pain.

Once she told you Alice, that the pain was unbearable and asked you to call the doctor to renew the prescription. Even then I didn't comprehend.

One special day sticks in my mind because it seemed as if she were coming back to normal. Bubble and I went up and I had fixed a tray of things she could eat—baked white chicken and grapes and oranges and cheese, all arranged prettily. We sat at the table and she ate some of everything and really enjoyed it. We weren't worried about her at that early stage—just concerned. Then she rested on the couch and talked to Bubble while I worked on an abstract montage of Gadie's face that I had brought with me. I was drawing his profile on black paper and inserting pictures of objects pertaining to him in his brain. She made a suggestion that I have popcorn coming out his ears because he liked popcorn so well. I think of her often when I look at that picture.

That day I took her a new dress I had gotten at Seymour's on sale. It was a lime green shirtwaist dress.

When we used to go shopping a long time ago she wore size sixteen dresses. She tried to lose weight and gradually got to where she could wear size fourteen. She was proud of that. She always wanted my opinion on what looked right and didn't trust her own.

At times, after she had gotten something on her own, she would ask my opinion and I would give it honestly. Once it was on a pair of black shoes which I didn't particularly like and I gave a noncommittal "Oh, they're alright" answer. From then on she didn't like those shoes even though she still wore them.

But this day the dress I brought her was a size too large. I exchanged it for a twelve. It fit except in the bust and she told me to take it back because "after she regained her weight it wouldn't fit."

But this day, as we prepared to leave, she got up from the couch and jokingly, yet also solemnly, came over and said "let me kiss you all goodbye" and she kissed us both. She had on her red flowered robe and I dismissed the seriousness of the kiss—pushed it from my mind.

I wanted to scream: "No—don't do that—don't get up from your sick bed and kiss me goodbye. Don't do anything different—let everything be the same. Always!"

You see—we never kissed Hello or Goodbye. Isn't that strange—I kiss or hug most other older family members everytime—but never her.

I don't know why—we were extremely close and had such a tremendous rapport—but we didn't show physical signs of our affection. We did on extremely serious occasions like my wedding day and before I would leave on long trips, but otherwise we didn't. That's why this last kiss was so symbolic.

Just recently, Lowell, you said she told you that her vital organs had just worn out. That was shortly before she went to the hospital evidently. How strange that a vital woman like Hash could ever get to that point without us ever suspecting the seriousness of it. Was she hiding so much for so long, or did it come upon her quickly?

I feel like the long hard winter of 77-78 took its deadly toll on her mind and body to a certain extent, and also the tumor reached its climax at that time. One worked with the other and both share the blame. Worry and frustration that accompany a harsh winter complicated things and perhaps hastened the decline of her health. If so, we could only be thankful that it was swift—none of us would have wanted her to have lingered on in pain, would we? To me that was the merciful aspect of the whole ordeal—the swiftness of it.

Going along with my theory of whether or not she knew reminds me of her calling me once during the very early stages, before I ever suspected anything, and laughing about the old song "Honey." She had just heard it and there is a part in there about the angels coming and carrying her away when she was there all alone. She said she got to thinking about that song and just laughed and laughed about the idea of the angels coming and carrying her away someday. That surely was a plea for me to listen to her and talk about that, wasn't it? Why didn't I catch the undertones of what she might have wanted to say?

That song had made quite an impression on her when it first came out years ago. I remember her telling me that we should really appreciate having our husbands or wives and think about how terrible it would be to lose them. The story is about a young wife dying and how her husband missed her.

Later she must have told James the same thing about laughing about the angels and the conversation must have gotten serious. I think at the time that James broke down and cried at things she said.

She told Ruth a time or two at home while she was having such a hard time that she would just rather be dead than to have to go through all that. She made it sound like such a logical choice and not a bit emotional—just a common-sense decision. She wasn't afraid of death it seems and that is what she would choose for herself, but not the grief for us.

I can see her telling that same thing to Gadie after she was out of intensive care and in the last room. She talked only to him and not once would she look at me as she said "You know, I would much rather to have died than to have gone through all that, not eating or not being able to have a drink of water." She avoided my eyes completely as she said that, but I was pleased that it was all spoken in the past tense as if it was behind her. Also, the fact that she mentioned the absence of food and drink, but not pain as what bothered her. That gave me some measure of comfort then.

When Gadie visited her in the unit, she made a shattering statement to him, even though she presented it in her characteristically silly way: "Now you won't be able to call me 'big greasy momma' anymore." Such a final statement, and yet it didn't seem so at the time.

But the event that more or less convinced me that she did know was the way she told Daddy goodbye. It was in the intensive care unit that terrible Sunday that I can never erase from my mind. How did we ever get through that day—expecting every minute to be the last and each short visit we were allowed in to look at her to be the last look. How I tried to imprint her face in my memory each time I walked backward from the room and how hard it was to go through the door—how final. The way it finally happened was so much easier—we were there and didn't have to wonder.

Mary Ann, you went in with Daddy and told Hash that he was there. She looked up and he held her hand and said a few words, then turned abruptly to leave before he lost control. As he got to the door she said "Goodbye Woodrow" and smiled the sweetest smile—calm and serene. Mary Ann, you said that she said it in the sweetest way imaginable and also in such a final way that after hearing her you never doubted that she meant just that—"Goodbye Woodrow"........

On the other hand, I at times feel that she didn't know and that she thought maybe she was wrestling with some infection in her body which would soon be cleared up. That's what I clung to at the doctors suggestion and maybe she did too.

The time we went to the emergency room in Lexington and the young doctor checked her and said it was evidently nothing but gall bladder trouble and everything else was alright was such a relief to us and to her. I grabbed the news like a drowning man clutching for a straw and accepted it fully. I feel like she did too at the moment because she said to me as I sat on the couch with her, "You know, I didn't know but what all my organs had given up at the same time." That was the very first time she ever voiced any concern to me and then it was as if in the past tense. Still that old protection there—sheltering me from worry.

Way back in the winter she said to Bubble, "You know, we just don't know what is going on in our bodies." A person in normal health probably wouldn't think of making a statement like that.

Going up to Shirley Downs once at a meeting, she started talking about the resurrection—more or less out of the blue—and said that the resurrection would be a wonderful thing for a person to experience, as if she herself expected to.

Perhaps she suspected, but wouldn't allow it put into words. Were we displaying the same oblivious attitude?

I now believe she knew things were bad, but rather than find out how bad, I believe she just drifted on away, choosing not to fight one way or another. That would be easy; I could do that.

She never asked us what the doctors were saying; she expressed neither hope nor worry. It was strange—as if her emotions were in limbo.

I always pictured her a fighter, but she didn't fight this. At first, I was disappointed in her in that respect, but then I realized that if she had fought it for awhile, her victory would have been a shallow one. Being the type of cancer that it was and considering its rapid development at the end, there was no hope. There are many types of cancer that do respond to treatment and a fight is necessary but the type of cancer that she had would not have responded to treatment at this stage. So a fight on her part would only have prolonged the painful battle and not one of us would have wanted that, would we?

Several times, she turned her face to the wall and feebly waved her hand, saying, "Just go on." Go on with what—go on with our lives? Let her go on with hers—on out........?

Did she know? Did she not? That's for her alone to answer.

# 6
# TEXTURE OF LIFE

In the grand pattern of life, I have found that her texture and mine ran the same. Numerous times I have seen the same threads running through our lives, weaving a similar pattern and design of living.

Noteworthy also is the fact that at many times our lifestyle was in direct contrast; there was as much difference as burlap and velvet.

Here I will dwell however on the similarities: the responses to life situations, the sense of humor, the artistic strain and the sentimentality.

As a young girl living in Lexington, where Poppa had a store, she said she would love to come in from school and have some Welch's Grape Juice (which is Tracy's delight now) and some cheese. Then she would put on her "artist smock" and paint pictures with great flourishing strokes.

Loving to paint myself, I can just imagine how she felt then. She drew constantly; mainly it was pictures of girls wearing beautiful dresses which she designed. I too did that all through school—there were more faces and eyes on my papers than lessons.

Somewhere during her early life her artistic nature submerged and as far as I know it never ever showed itself again. I can't remember her having the slightest interest in any form of art. I wonder what happened.

The same thing almost happened to me. The interest in such things carried over into my early married life and the first four or five years I painted with a passion—all abstract art. (Now that is the art form I am least interested in.)

However, after Scarlett was born I lost all interest in such things, and not until she was twelve or thirteen years old did I rekindle my interest. Art lessons with Judy Apple were started and with her expert guidance and enthusiasm I now enjoy painting more than ever before.

Her studio is called Apple's Alley and Jessee Stewart and I paint together there; I love to paint portraits. Now the strain is following through and Scarlett and Tracy both go with me for lessons. It is marvelous.

Virginia Warth recently mentioned the book called "Silences" which deals with this very thing—people suddenly drop their artistic projects and take time off for various reasons such as raising families, etc. Then these talents resurface years later and are followed on through.

Hash's death found me so full of unspoken words and emotions I felt I would burst if I could not expell some of them. But the idea of writing them on paper never occured to me until one day at the farm when there was no one else there but little Shane. We had been gathering pine cones and I was sitting on the porch, remembering....

## Autumn of Tears

Sitting on the crumbling old porch with the golden leaves crunching beneath my feet, I wondered about the troubled thoughts tumbling through my head.

The sadness, which comes always with the dying of the summer, was so much different this time.

As I picked up the weathered old basket I have brought out to gather some of the precious souvenirs of the sweet by-gone summer-leaves, faded flowers and pine cones—I picture tired, lined old hands, weary with age, which must have held this old basket many, many times.

Then I remember that my mother's hands never became feeble and shaky—they were still firm and capable when she went away from us.

I sit transfixed with the unbearable hurt that this is the first autumn of my life without her...and the leaves fall faster, swirls of russet and bronze...bewildering me.

The mellow sun, like melted butter in autumns past, now grows dim as I acknowledge the fact that she will never see my son grow into the seasons of a man or see the slowly developing grace of a special child.

Also, my mind rebells against the knowledge that she'll not come back to us with the spring flowers nor with the summer sun—not at all until her season is complete. Until then, I'll remain forever in the winter of her life.

I'm not really sure but I believe she said she wrote poetry then. That's what I love to do, only I write prose. I don't like to have to search for a rhyming word which I might not feel—I just like to let the words ramble.

"Words" meant a lot to her as they do to me, and probably to most of you. Lowell, you are the exception, being a "mincer" of words, and Alice falls not too far behind.

But Hash loved words and knew the meaning of almost all words that she came in contact with. How I used to marvel at that. I remember asking her once, "How do you know all those words and what they mean?"

One day Scarlett asked me that same question about myself, and I laughed because even though I do know a lot of words, I also am an expert at butchering other words which I'm not too familiar with.

Once, to give you an example, I mentioned to Hash that the "Glass Menagerie" was going to be on TV, only I pronounced it "Menagree". She laughed and laughed at that until she realized that I was serious. (then she laughed even more)

As a child, I fondly recall her reciting the Greek alphabet, going faster and faster as she reached the end, like a roller coaster. I suppose the knowledge of Latin helped her tremendously in her understanding of words.

She would sit and read by the hour and I am sure that her ability to lose herself in a book helped her through some of the more difficult years of her life. Books are an escape many times, as I'm sure you know.

I read very little now; my spare time is used to paint or write. In fact, none of us have ever been the voracious reader she was, and she read to such an extent that in my minds eye she and books are inseparable.

Mary Ann, I remember telling you that she said "I love to get a good book and sit down and read, read, read, read, read!"

In the summers of my childhood I had what you might "almost" call an insatiable desire for the Little Colonel books. They were introduced to me by Hash, she having read them when she was a young girl; I in turn introduced Scarlett to them with the same eagerness she had conveyed to me. These are the threads tying our lives together that I mentioned.

"Anne of Green Gables" was in the same time period—Anne with an E. Last summer at the Flea Market an old book caught my eye. It was "Anne of Avonlea"—another in the series of "Anne" books. Whether or not I read it back then I don't remember, but Scarlett latched on to it right away and I could see myself sitting there devouring it all over again as she commented on what a good book it was.

"Pollyanna" was with us through our girlhood, and I hope you young generation of girls—Marjorie and Cheryl and Rachel—will go to the library and check out a few of these "books of old" which enriched our young lives—thanks to Hash.

Before I leave the subject of books, I want to tell you about Hash and her cousin Jesse and "The Shiek".

We are bombarded with more blantant sex in one mouth wash commercial today than that entire book held, but Hash said she and Jesse would hide up in the loft of the barn and read it together, shivering with the sheer excitement of it and giggling all the while.

Books wielded great influence over her life, and she would quote from different ones, recalling funny episodes as if they were family history.

One book that highly impressed her and seemed to help her through a difficult period of her life was "The Power of Positive Thinking". Being very young at the time, I can nevertheless remember the, pardon the pun, very positive tone she used when she spoke admiringly of that book.

Books certainly can influence your life, can't they? Mine has been influenced by "Gone With the Wind". Scarlett, of course, being the most obvious influence and wanting to name the farm Tara, but also the fascination of a red slip (mainly the appreciation of Hash's fascination) and of hospitality and of long lost charming ways.

Hash was reading a novel just before Tiffany was born and the heroine's name was Chantel. Scarlett mentioned to you, Mary Ann, that Hash said how pretty that would be for you to use if you had a girl. So when you did have "a girl" you called here for me to check the book to see what "that name" was. I found the book, related the name to you and thus Tiffany Chantel was "born".

It was a wonderful thing that Hash got to see little Tiffany and I know how thankful you are for that, Mary. After she was born in December, Alice and Kay, Hash, Bubble and I came up to see her the first week in January and then in February you and Tiffany stayed all night with her. You have those moments to remember and to be thankful for, Mary.

Of all the books which have influenced her life, none of course compares to the Bible. She was more familiar with and knowledgeable about it than anyone I've ever met. I honestly believe that there wasn't a question you could ask pertaining to the Bible that she couldn't answer.

Anything that you are highly interested in you can retain easily; she retained every word she ever read in the Bible, in my estimation.

I miss calling her now as I used to do whenever a question was brought up pertaining to names or genealogies or lineage—she would have the answer as quick as a wink.

Not only in those respects, but she also had a clear-cut understanding of the doctrines. At times, listening to her, you might not be too sure about the "clear-cut" aspect, considering the fact that her presentation of it was at times hard to follow, what with her rapid fire delivery and intense desire to get it *ALL* across to you at once! Remember how she talked with her hands—I suppose if her hands had been cut off she wouldn't have been able to speak a word!

She could be as eloquent and coherent as anyone when she set her mind to it, but usually she spoke with her heart and not one of us would have wanted her to be any different, would we?

That one quality is what I believe endeared her to so many people—her straight-forward interest in them—her intense desire to tell them that they too could have the chance to live forever in a paradise condition. Being so full of zeal in this respect, she took every opportunity to tell it to others, and each time it almost seemed to be the first to her. Often I have prayed to have the same zeal she had—I admired that quality in her more than any other.

The first thing she would do most mornings after she ate was to sit down on the couch and read either the Bible or books related to the Bible. She would become totally absorbed in whatever it was, and often even forgot the time.

Being the proud possessor of one of her old Bibles (She went through them quickly, wearing them out with her constant use), I often leaf through it, seeing the familiar passages marked by pencil, and at those times I am so grateful that I can say that she was greatly influenced by "the book".

Following through on my theme of the "Texture of Life", I remember that her life was shot through with threads of sentimentality. Being a sentimental woman, she took things to heart, and was often hurt or upset by such things. But this is just a part of life.

She didn't worry about big things—those were the things that would "work out". What she did worry about was people; people who were neglected, people who were alone, people who were sad, and children who were hungry.

Animals were of interest to her and the fact that Gadie and Scarlett and Tracy always seemed to be adding something new to our "menagree" was a constant source of concern to her, considering the high mortality rate which she kept note of.

When Tracy's cat, Princess, was run over and had to have brain surgery, staying in the veterinarian's hospital for two days, we made sure we kept the news from Hash until it was back home. (Come to think of it, we kept the news from Gadie too, but for a different reason.)

When one of our ostriches escaped and I put a "lost" ad in the paper, I hoped she wouldn't hear about it until it was found. (This story about the ostrich "Rodeo" is too priceless to leave out—I must tell it.) All three ostriches broke out of their enclosure one day and the great chase was on! Gadie gave chase in the jeep, with Larry and Harlan in full pursuit in back-up trucks and some of the men were on foot.

Just as they would start to gain ground and pull up beside them, one of those big birds would, in Harlan's words: "shift it into third gear and spin on out!" It was a fantastic chase—nothing compares to the speed of an ostrich—and I love the story! Lassoes were considered, but there was no time. They must be captured before they got out on the road! There would be no stopping them then!

Motorists coming down Lemons Mill were seen to shake their heads and rub their eyes, knowing that they didn't really see an ostrich, or was it a road runner, streaking along on the other side of that fence. And why were those wild looking men running and shouting and waving their hats? Such strange "goings on" on that hill...peacocks screaming at night and some people swear it sounds more like a woman...and now this wild scene!

•

Remember the two darling twin baby goats we had—darling ONLY when they were very small—and one broke it's leg while jumping over a gate to get to our tender young tree sprouts? Gadie set its leg and put a cast on it and it was just fine, but Hash worried about it all the time.

Gadie went downtown and bought jewelry for them—a pink necklace and pierced earrings for the little white one and red necklace and pierced earrings for the black one. Then Scarlett took them to the classroom at her school and the principal had her take them around to every room for all the kids to see.

Hash thought it was terrible that Gadie pierced their ears, but they didn't mind at all.

Who will ever forget Bojangles, the enormous pet bull we loved? Scarlett raised him from a calf on a bottle and he just walked around in our yard like a dog and never left—except once.

He left then because Gadie highly insulted him. We kept him in the garage every night, but this particular night he rambled around and knocked over every bucket and everything that would rattle and bang. The poor thing must have had colic, because usually he slept quietly all night. I can still see Gadie, grumpy from loss of sleep, outlined against the light in his undershorts and tall boots, giving Bojangles a swift kick out of the garage right on his rump roast! The next morning he was gone, and Gadie went all over the neighborhood searching for him, but to no avail.

After giving up, he started home and to his surprise, there was Bojangles snuggled up on the porch of the house next door to us, looking like a petulant child. But he grew...and he grew! He would still, when almost full grown, stretch out on the ground and lay his massive head in Scarlett's lap. I have pictures of that. But finally, when he grew too fond of breaking ribs and tossing people up into the air, we had no alternative but to sell him. How we tried to keep that news from Hash and we did for quite awhile.

Then there was the pig who thought he was a dog! Remember Larry's pig, "Gaylord", who was raised with our dog "Cimmaron" and lived in the dog house and ate dog food? This too was in town, with no fence needed to keep him in. No wonder the neighbors thought we were the Beverly Hillbilly's. When he became full grown he too was enormous and I have hilarious movies of all the kids riding him, especially Lindsay Clay. He looked like a wild young Indian riding a greased pig. He too had to go the way of all good pets, via the market, but we never told Hash about him.

One day Gadie brought in an old bony nag named Countess Way, and we took "before and after" pictures of her to see how she improved as she was cared for by Scarlett. Hash never neglected to ask about her and she worried about that poor old horse like you wouldn't believe!

Tracy periodically brings little mice home; for some reason field mice seem much cleaner than house mice, and I don't mind them at all. Just last month, he went down to the lake and when he turned the row boat over, there was a little pitiful looking mouse, shivering and cold. So of course, he brought it home, put it in a nice warm box, and of course it was out of the box and gone the next morning....

Our most well-known mouse was named Bojangles. It too was a field mouse. Tracy was about four years old and he had been out all afternoon with Gadie. He went to sleep in the car and when Gadie carried him in and laid him on his bed, something soft and gray slipped out of his pocket—it was a mouse! We fed it with an eye-dropper and after eating, it would take both tiny paws or hands and wipe it's little mouth—adorable. It slept in a woven basket about the size of an egg; can you believe I would get up and give it a two-o'clock feeding every morning? Tracy drove it around the floor in his tiny Match Box jeep; it seemed to enjoy the rides. But finally it died— from car sickness! We hated to tell Hash.

The animal she loved dearly was that mangy little poodle of hers-Gi Gi. Alice, you gave it to her, probably having no idea how attached to it she would become and it became almost like a child to her—and to James.

Speaking of her sentimental streak makes me remember a time not many years ago when I asked her to write down a poem she was quoting from called "The Old School House". Not knowing all of it, she looked it up in the library and wrote it down for me. I still have it. Several months later she mentioned that after she had relived all those memories through the poem, she had been overcome with the most terrible depression that lasted for a long time.

Poetry didn't usually effect her that way however; I can remember her quoting and reciting so many things over the years. Many of my enjoyments today are influenced by snatches of memory and patchworks of rememberances which have filtered down from my childhood.

Indians are very important to me—I enjoy Indian designs and their culture and their way of life. Tracing the pattern back, thread by thread, I discovered the fascination I have for Indians stems from the magical way Hash used to tell us the story of "Hiawatha". I can still hear the exciting way she would say: "By the shores of Gitche Gumee, by the shining Big-Sea-Water, stood the wigwam of Nokomis', Daughter of the Moon, Nokomis." I can remember Little Laughing Waters and Wah-wah-taysee and all the others. We would be overwhelmed by the beauty of it (at least I would) and it made a lasting impression on me.

For some time I didn't understand why I bought, at an auction, on the spur of the moment, an old oil painting of two Indians standing on a hill— for ninety dollars! Gradually I realized that the name of the painting, "Hiawatha's Wedding" was what did me in.

Yes, all these memories and thoughts are interwoven in my mind, creating a pattern that I live by. Needless to say, all these are knotted together by means of a "scarlet" cord. That applied to Hash and to me—she loved Scarlett so and she said there was always something "special" about Scarlett. I'm so glad she thought so because so did I.

Speaking of Scarlett reminds me of one distinguishable thread running through our life, albeit a twisted thread; it is dancing and the love of dancing or the lack of the love of dancing or the lackadaisical love of dancing. What do you mean, you are confused? Just let me explain.

You see, Hash loved dancing. She could have been a professional, I'm sure, had she trained for it. I always wondered why she didn't since Poppa could have afforded it. Perhaps dancing lessons weren't available then; perhaps she wasn't interested. However, once she danced on stage at Oxford School in some little talent show.

But I remember when we first started watching television, down at Uncle Tom's store. Wasn't that the greatest thing when all of Muddy Ford would congregate at the store on Saturday night and sit in rows of straight chairs or benches in front of that shiny new television? We were all spellbound—fascinated at this newfangled "thing".

We watched wrestling matches with "Argentina Rocco" and "Snooky Lansen" and "Hit Parade", etc. I remember Hash saying how she hated to even watch the dancers because, as she said: "I could be doing that". That is the only time I can remember her ever saying that something "might have been" and seeming to have regrets.

Being agile and extremely well-coordinated she would have indeed made an outstanding dancer, as we could see when she did her celebrated "Charleston". How we loved to get her to do it—all the grandchildren begged her to show them how. (Little Rachel thought that when she would cross her hands back and forth over her knees so fast she was trying to "cover" herself!)

I remember when she and Daddy used to go to square dances or "barn dances" and how she enjoyed them. Once a little "strange" woman came up to her and patted her and said "I think you're pretty". Then she asked her to dance with her. With the greatest amazement Hash naively said of her, "Do you know, I believe there must have been something funny about her!" She never understood things like that about people.

Back to dancing, she loved it and regreted that she did nothing about it; I love it but never expect to "do" anything about it; Scarlett "does" something about it weekly, but doesn't love it. Now, what do you make of all that?

Scarlett has taken ballet, tap and jazz and toe dancing over the years since she was four years old. It was always my fondest dream to have a little girl who could toe dance. However, before you jump to the conclusion that I forced her "up on her toes", that's not true. Even though I probably do live out my childhood fantasies when I see her on the stage with a spot light on her, I have never pushed her to keep up her lessons. She took off a year or two from dancing because she felt like she wanted a change, and I never argued that point at all. She went back when she was ready.

I went one day last week and watched her rehearse, just she and her teacher, Artie Janow, in front of the full length mirror and to me it was the most exciting thing imaginable. All of it was: the music, the routine, the ballet steps, the discipline of "the dance"; to Scarlett it was just a lesson. Life is ironic, wouldn't you say?

Now I too have started taking classes at the same studio—the Dance Theater. Mine are a combination of dance and exercise and I enjoy it so much. When I am wearing a leotard and tights and doing ballet exercises at the barre I feel invigorated, intrepid, insouciant, involved, insuperable, but when I am trying to dance, one word describes me—inept!

One thing I am glad for is that Hash never missed any of Scarlett's dance recitals—none of her piano recitals—she didn't even miss her debut at birth! She was right there at Scarlett's and Tracy's birth and I'm glad.

Speaking of not missing a recital reminds me of the fact that Gadie's little mother never missed one either. She was at all the important occasions and thoroughly enjoyed it all. She lived her little life to the fullest. Hash said of her, "There's not a day goes by that I don't think of that little woman".

Back to dancing, the kind of dancing I love the most is folk dancing. It's so exciting! Doris Clark and I went not too long ago to see the Russian Folk Dancers and how fabulous they were! The high leaps and twirls and the fabulous leg work! I enjoyed it immensely, but my enjoyment was tinged with sadness because I thought of Hash all through the program and how she would have loved the excitement of it. She used to crouch down with her arms crossed and try to do that difficult step of kicking out first one leg and then the other.

If she had been there, she would have been thinking: "I could do that".

One of the greatest nights I can remember was when Gadie and Alice and I went to a "Grecian Festival" in Lexington. We ate all the natural food and drank ouzo, then watched their special style of entertainment. At the end, a lot of people got up and danced the folk dance, the Handkerchief Dance, encouraging everyone to join in. Alice and I got up and tried it and I loved it so. I had on a long red dress and I kicked off my shoes and we all danced in a circle, holding hands. I enjoyed it so; I want to go to Greece.

On the subject of Grecian customs, I fulfilled the desire I always had of flinging a wine glass against the wall. There were a lot of people at our house and I called them all into the den, then I flung my wine glass against the rock wall around the fireplace! (The glass was made of plastic though; somehow the effect was lost.)

Always before, when I did something I enjoyed, I could call Hash and share it with her. Now I can't, and how I miss that camaraderie. I shared everything with her. In fact, when I first became pregnant (she was with me when the doctor confirmed the news) I was so happy and told her one of the reasons I wanted to have a baby was so she could enjoy it too.

When Scarlett was born, she and Lillian had been with me from the onset; all the others came a little later. All along she had been upbeat and relaxed about me having a baby, but just after they got me settled in the labor room, a worried look came over her face and she said, "Oh, now that it is about to start, I really hate to see you have to go through this".

What timing—what tact! I've always been surprised at her saying such a thing.

Dancing reminds me of singing. In this pattern and design of life, she was not "cut out" to sing. Neither were we. None of us can sing, can we? In a way, that seems rather sad. I never thought much about it until the time when Lilly, a girl who lived in one of our little tenant houses, made a comment on it. However, she was talking about her husband when she said, "He and his family never sang. I can't imagine such a thing as a family never singing!"

At the meeting we would look at each other, Hash, Scarlett and I, and get tickled at our total lack of musical ability. Hash would roll her eyes around and if I was sitting next to her, she would always come out really strong on the very last word of a song.

That is all so vivid, can it be she is really gone? I cannot comprehend it. The meetings are so hard for me; she was a part of the meetings. She was always there. I hear a song, read a favorite scripture, see a fleeting expression and it all comes back to me. It's so hard.

Back to the music—we were not a total loss however. I'm sure all of you except Alice (you were just a baby) remember when Daddy would get us all on his knees and say "Alright now, let's show Buddy Drake a thing or two!"

Then we would sing all the hymns we knew at the top of our voice! I mean, so loud it would burst your eardrums! Buddy Drake, our neighbor, would sing hymns at the top of his voice as he went about his work and occasionally Daddy decided we should do the same and it was great fun.

Mary Ann, how could we ever forget the time Miss Rose, our music teacher, called us into the music room at Oxford and had us stand on each side of the piano and sing as she played? We could never figure out the purpose of it, could we? Was she (God forbid) considering having us sing on a program or was she judging us for a music grade? Whatever the reason, I'll never forget the memorable words she uttered after we finished: "Now, don't ever let anyone tell me the Fields girls can't sing!" My insides laughed so hard at that; behold—the melodious Field's sisters!

In conclusion then, all the aspects of our lives have woven together for good or for bad, forming somewhat of a cloak to cover ourself with—a cloak of memories. It's as warm as a smile, as soft as a kiss and it will never fade—I wrap it around me to ward off the chill of sadness.

So then, all the years of our lives, the past, present and future (of which she is very much a part) are stitched together with the silver thread of memories. Our lives are a patchwork of experiences, trials and joys, each unique yet blending together in the end to form one harmonious whole.

# 7
# SHE FELT LIKE CRYING

If I ever saw her cry, my mind won't let me remember it. I don't think I could have stood to see her cry.

But that is a mistake—to be so ashamed to cry and to be seen crying. I don't know how I ever got that way and I wish it wasn't so because crying is good and natural and to be encouraged.

Once I said to someone, in reply to their comment about needing a good cry, that I hadn't cried in years and I was proud of it I suppose. I was proud of my control. It's a wonder I didn't develop arthritis or ulcers, etc.

But now I cry all the time, about Hash, but still I would be horrified to be so weak as to cry in front of certain people. I never let Gadie see me cry; I never really let anyone "see" me cry. I run and hide my weakness. Many times at night I have laid with my head on Gadie's shoulder and cried even though he never knew it. I don't know why I am so reluctant to let him share my grief; I know he would be able to sympathize.

If I died and people looked through my belongings, everything they found would be so personal and sad and significant because I save so many "words and pictures and things". I'll tear out a beautiful picture I someday want to paint, I'll jot down a combination of words that fit together and I'll save a picture of a marvelous face from a magazine because I like the lines in the face.

But Hash's life seemed strangely bare of "things". I hadn't thought of it until now, but she didn't seem to be a very "personal" woman. I guess another way of saying that is she didn't seem to have anything to hide or to be private about.

In contrast, I am completely private and turn inward from the world. (Why then, you're asking, am I now bearing myself to the world?) I don't know.

The only things she had that could be called private and personal were her books. Even there, you could find no clues as to her inner self because the books were the same books that all of Jehovah's Witnesses have.

The books that she read otherwise, and there were many, were all borrowed from the library and returned, so they couldn't be called personal. In contrast, I have a small collection of books and in looking through them you could tell the story of my life from my selection.

What I am driving at is that there are such few momentos to identify with her and to cling to.

Considering this, Mary Ann and Alice and I looked through her books and her drawers, hoping against hope to find some clue as to whether she knew what was happening or whether it came upon her as suddenly as it did upon us.

Mary Ann, you said you just wish she had written some little notes and stuffed them here and there—how happy we would have been to have found them.

But no, there was nothing. In the drawer where all her pictures were, (and what a treasure old pictures are), there was a little note scribbled about being scared of the test Dr. Wells made.

Then James found this sad little entry in her Bible and it broke our hearts:

January 21—felt like crying
February 12

Just that—no explanation and no follow up.

I would have felt so much worse about it, being a non-cryer and unable to understand this lonely feeling, but Mary Ann, you explained it to me so well.

You, being so much like her, told me that over the years you too just felt like crying at different times and for no reason. You said it helps a lot to "have a good cry" and get it over with—until the next time.

Once, after her divorce from Daddy, I was playing a sad song by Elvis and Mary Ann, you told me not to play it anymore because it made Hash cry.

There must have been many times she wanted to talk and express her fears, but she never did; did she think we would fall apart? I really wish I could have helped her then, but she never divulged any fear or doubts at all on the matter.

When she felt like crying, I wonder if she did?

# 8
# DIDN'T WE ALL
# ENJOY THE ROLLS?

Hash was an excellent "maker of rolls." All my life I can remember her rolling out the dough, folding each roll over in a particular way and then when they were finished, how delicious they were! One special treat was when she would make the second pan into cinnamon rolls—nothing was ever as delectable.

She enjoyed doing that for us—she got genuine enjoyment from our delight, the same delight I get now from fixing Tracy a cherry pie.

Friends were often the recipients of her spontaneous roll-making, as was I.

When we were all young, she belonged to the Homemaker Club. They would meet at different homes each time and everyone would bring a dish; as far as I remember she was always asked to bring rolls.

That reminds me of the time they were to meet at our house, when we lived on the hill with Mommau. A great flurry of cleaning and polishing and shining was finally accomplished and then came the day for the ladies to meet. The kitchen window was steamed up that morning from the cooking, so with my finger I wrote on the window: "The Homemakers are coming today!" Hash was too busy to notice it until the day was over and then, as now, I was surprised at her reaction. She actually seemed mortified to think that maybe some of them noticed my proclamation (it was visible all day) but she also seemed amused at her mortification. After all her thorough window cleaning it was all offset by, of all people, sweet little Fannee, "who never did anything wrong."

Once we were having company, about five years ago, and Hash made a beautiful pan of rolls for us. They were highly appreciated by all—the only highpoint of the meal—and I decided to call her on the phone and have

everyone shout, in unison, their approval after I asked the question—
"Didn't we all enjoy the rolls?" I believe Doug and Sue and Judy and Bob
and their families were here and our appreciation was obvious to her.

I first "coined the phrase" of "Didn't we all enjoy the rolls" after a
Sunday dinner we had at her house. Mary Ann, you and Nelson and the kids
were there as was Alice and Shane and Gadie and Larry, Scarlett, Tracy and
I. I even happen to have pictures of that little occasion.

Now, Mary Ann, you are carrying on her roll-making tradition, aren't
you? You found her recipe which she had written out for you, never
needing to look at it herself, of course, and you worked at it until you had it
perfected; until it tasted just like hers. When you achieved that same taste,
you sent me one through the mail to proclaim your victory. Please keep it
up—teach Rachel to make rolls like Hash.

Alice, almost every Sunday she had you and Shane come up, didn't
she? She really loved to cook those chicken and noodles or a roast and green
beans and macaroni salad. People need someone to cook for, someone who
appreciates good food, and she wanted you all to come. I know how badly
you felt later, when you said she got up and cooked that last month for you
when she obviously felt bad. But as Mary Ann told you, she wanted to do it
and you should be so glad you let her; it was what she wanted to do.

The kids declared that she made the "best hamburgers in the world"
and she would jump up and make popcorn for them at the mere hint of the
word.

None of the five of us can forget our favorite meal when we were little,
I'm sure. What was it? It was before we knew the perils and the pitfalls of
starches, and horrors, two starches together!

Right—macaroni and fried potatoes! How we loved it! The macaroni
was just plain and mixed with ketchup and the taste of it with the fried
potatoes was delightful; nothing that I fix evokes the same response from
Scarlett and Tracy, except possibly lobster.

Hash fixed that meal often, to say the least, and each time the word
would echo through the house from one kid to the other: "macaroni and
potatoes for supper!"

In fact, it was such an all time favorite with you Lowell, that you asked
her to bring it to you when you were in the hospital once. Remember? I
don't know if she was able to swing that or not, but I imagine she did if it
was allowed. She always tried to oblige us in every way.

Of course, you also remember what treat there was in the skillet of fried
potatoes, I'm sure. The big toe! She would cut one piece of potato extra
large and we all clamored to be the one to find that "big toe."

That little oddity came from that old story Poppa used to tell called
"Scabby-Headed Jack" when the question was asked of everyone as to
whether they wanted "big toe or bacon." We all wanted "big toe."

The kitchen of that house evidently looms heavily on my
subconsciousness because I have dreamed about it numerous times and I
remember so much about it.

A woman's kitchen tells a lot, doesn't it? Her whole personality is laid out before you in a kitchen, as Mary Ann says. That is, unless she is the type to sweep it all back in the far corner of her cabinets, then close the doors tightly so you can't see her at all.

Hash never tried to hide much, as far as I know. She was what she was, with very few pretenses.

Her kitchen in that house was symbolic of my childhood, I believe. I dream so often of events occurring as I look out that window—the one facing the road. I have dreamed of things happening in the yard in front of the window and to the side of it—where that old plum tree stood. Something or some things, very traumatic or else extremely pleasant surely have occurred right there for it to figure so dramatically in my subconsciousness. I wish I knew.

There was a round pedestal table, always covered with an oilcloth, and a kitchen cabinet to the right; it was like the one Gadie got for our house at the farm. It had the flour and sugar bins and it was white, trimmed in red. Then to the left of the table was a floor to ceiling cabinet, built into the wall. There she kept cereal and crackers among other things.

Then there was the cooking stove, (electric) and the woodbox behind the little pot-bellied heating stove and on the other wall the table with the bucket of water with the dipper in it.

On that little table is where I washed my hair and she told me to rinse it "until it squeaked." (My hair hasn't squeaked like that in years.)

At times, Daddy would decide to make chocolate milk. He would take an enormous jar and after filling it with milk and the appropriate chocolate mixture, he would sit and shake it vigorously between his big hands for what seemed like an eternity while all of us gathered around in a tight little knot, a knot which grew tighter as our anticipation grew. That chocolate milk was hard to "come by" back then.

Since this chapter is predominantly about culinary memories, in case you haven't noticed, I must mention the oatmeal memories that Mary Ann and I have.

We were the first ones on the school bus in the morning and the last off in the evening. The only factor in our favor was that we could sit right behind the driver, where the heater was, and don't think we ever relinquished that privilege! We had a kindly driver, John Lewis Corbin, who would wait for us in the morning to come tumbling out of the house and in the evening he would again wait while one or the other of us might run in the house to see if we could ride on "down to Momma's." He was so kind—he's dead now or I would tell him so.

In the mornings we would be stuffed *full* of hot oatmeal; we would often be stuffed into our coat and "leggings" simultaneously. Now that is a lethal combination and resulted often in Mary Ann's forced stopping of the school bus. She would have to get out to relieve herself of most of the oatmeal and she would wait beside the road for Kay to come along on her way to school, hitching a ride with her.

Kay was a life-saver many times back then, wasn't she? We would never have made it without her and I'm so grateful for her interest and support of us through the years. Thank you Kay—I really do appreciate all you were to us.

I remember the chocolate cakes Hash whipped up so effortlessly and how they delighted us. I remember even more the "one egg" cakes she specialized in. I never understood their significance—I still don't.

Most of my memories seem to center around the years that we lived in the old log cabin above Kay's. Perhaps that was my happiest time; Daddy told me that it definitely was for him.

Chocolate cake and red jello with bananas was our Sunday dessert then and how special it seemed!

One day, just before we ate, I happened upon a baby rabbit in it's death agony; what caused it I don't remember, but I watched it twitching until it died. Then at the table I couldn't eat that red jello and I sat transfixed, remembering. To my surprise, Hash asked me what was bothering me, and I was surprised that she knew something was wrong. I think she asked me about the rabbit and if it was hurt and even way back then, when I was so young, I wanted to "spare her feelings," so I said, "No, nothing is wrong." I remember exactly where I was sitting—and how I felt.

Do you remember Chicky Little, the white pet chicken that used to ride on top of my head? One day it just went over in Buz Feeback's place and never came back. Wonder what he had for Sunday dinner that week?

Who can ever forget the nest of baby mice we found and the nasty bald pinkness of them, with their eyes still closed? Mary Ann, you and I marvel now at the fiendish way we "did away with them." We went to the creek and actually held them under by the tails till they quit squirming. I can't believe that! But we did it; it was the first and last time I ever hurt anything deliberately.

Remember Brownie and Skipper? Skipper, the beautiful collie and Brownie, the mongrel—how we took sides over them and proclaimed each to be the best! Poor old Moon and Twinkle-toes, our cats—Moon with the lifeless tail dragging the ground and big gray Twinkle-toes. Then there was Old Tom, the Atom Bomb, an enormous tom cat that came and went with the greatest arrogance.

Daddy would bring in a gunny sack full of popping corn still on the cob, and what fun we would have shelling and popping it! Scarlett and Tracy never heard of popcorn being in that form, having only seen it in little bags or jars as we buy it now.

We had a constant supply of popcorn back then and Hash told me that was when she first started putting on weight. (Now I seldom eat popcorn—except at the movies. Some lessons are not to be ignored.)

Women didn't wear pants then; can it be possible that there was such a time? However Hash had a pair of bluejeans! I wonder where in the world she got them. They weren't mens—they zipped on the side, so that eliminates them being Daddy's. Oh, she enjoyed them so and wore them every day, it seems, even though she wouldn't have worn them outside the house for anything.

While I'm telling you about her pants, I'll tell about mine, lest I forget. Little girls always wore dresses then, and we were no exception. Hash took pride in dressing us; dresses could be neither too long nor too short. Even now, the most pitiful thing to see is a little girl with a long dress on, one that her mother didn't take time to hem after someone gave it to her. Right, Mary? Of course, that doesn't apply now with the long dresses that even little girls favor; they're easily recognizable from the "neglected hem" though.

Our first grade teacher was Mrs. Louise Adams and to my advantage she had a niece; to my further advantage the niece had glorious clothes. Mrs. Adams would give us, periodically, boxes of beautiful clothes as the niece outgrew them. I, being the oldest girl (oops, what am I revealing) was therefore blessed with a fine wardrobe, earning for me in school the nickname of "teacher's pet" because as one poor little girl said, "I had such pretty clothes."

To the point now: I too had pants! Pants, which little girls never wore! These however, were more than pants—they were stylish wool "riding pants!" Fitted with zippers at the bottom and flared at the hips—how cosmopolitan I must have looked—and only in the third grade! Thank you, Mrs. Adam's niece, wherever you are!

How many pieces have you ever divided a candy bar into? One of the hardest things for me to understand when I was little was why Hash never wanted a piece of candy when she divided one up for us! She would cut a Milky Way into five pieces and I honestly remember my genuine amazement as to why she never ever wanted a piece herself! She never made any issue over it and never made it seem a strange thing to do—dividing a candy bar five ways—and because of that we accepted it as normal too. When did any of you grandchildren ever divide a candy bar—even two ways? Think about it.

A mother has the ability to either make children feel deprived or to teach them to accept their circumstances as perfectly normal. Hash did the latter; perhaps she even did it unconsciously. I wouldn't say she tried to bolster us up and make things seem something they weren't—she just accepted things and we picked up that same attitude. Now perhaps some of you didn't accept it that way, but I did. I have nothing but happy memories of my childhood—they are all good. I know I have the ability to reject with my mind any unpleasantness and maybe I did, but I didn't knowingly do so. I really did have a wonderful childhood.

One classic example of accepting and making the best of what we had concerns a meal of a baked potato. Yes—a baked potato—period. It was a long time before I realized how unusual that was. I was remembering a time in the winter when it was too cold in the kitchen to eat, so Hash put potatoes in the oven to bake, then carried them into the room where it was warm for us to eat. She buttered each one liberally and mashed it up and it was delectable!

As I said, not until years later did it dawn on me that a potato alone is not a meal, but the manner in which she prepared them and presented them to us with such a flourish made it seem quite special. If, to the contrary, she had apologized as she gave them to us, I would perhaps have felt deprived and remembered the incident with a completely different feeling. Always be grateful for what you have.

By the way, did you know that the only real difference between a week of fasting and a week of starvation is "the stress" involved?

Early in the morning, before the sheep came out from the barn to the apple tree, she would hurry out and gather all the Grimes Golden apples that had fallen overnight and make the most glorious pies. Nothin' says lovin'........

At the farm, when I go out early in the morning to gather the pears which fall overnight, before the peacocks and turkeys start to peck at them, I am Hash.......I run barefoot through the dew; she wore shoes. I pass the swimming pool on the way to the tree; she reached the tree before going to the spring for a bucket of water.

Outward differences, yes, but inside, where it matters, we are the same.

Only one summer did we children have to work in tobacco. Lowell and Billy, I'm sure you all must have helped Daddy many summers, but there was only one where he elicited the help of all of us. It was when we lived up by Kay's house. I remember the tobacco patch in front of the house; Daddy was setting with a hand setter and we were running back and forth with small (to match us) buckets of water.

Then, when we were working in a distant field, Hash would come in the middle of the hot afternoon, bearing Alice, and more importantly, bearing ice water and fudge! That was her contribution to our break— fudge. How we enjoyed it!

Daddy never expected Hash to work in the fields and this was a testimony to "the aura of lady" that was always a part of her. I'm so glad of that.

"Momma's doing peaches, all the afternoon." Do you remember hearing that poem? I'll have to ask Uncle Pal who that is by so I can look it up and read it. He'll know, for sure.

Daddy went to Georgia and got a load of peaches. This was when he was doing a lot of trucking, hauling hay and corn.

Lowell, would you by any chance remember the fuzz on those peaches and if so, was it itchy? Just thought I would ask, but maybe you would rather forget the whole thing, considering that it took you several weeks to get all the fuzz washed off, along with the accompanying itch.

Hash sat on the back porch, peeling and cutting up those peaches, readying them to can. Nothing ever tasted as good as those peach slices we would reach for. She didn't seem to care how many we ate—she was just glad she had them for us.

Of course, there was a little peach tree right beside the porch where she was working, but they were not to be compared to those "Georgia peaches."

Besides, there was more worm than there was peach in ours, even though that didn't usually deter us, anymore than it did when we ate mulberries or wild cherries or blackberries. Oh, what healthy little animals we must have been, the worms notwithstanding. I feel blessed when I recall my childhood—I really do.

So now, after looking back, I can hear, as if it were reverberating through the years the answer to my question: "Didn't we all enjoy her *roles*"—Her roles as wife, sister, grandmother and most of all, as mother.

# 9
# OUR DESPERATE QUEST

A good starting point for this chapter will be December of 1977. The location was our house at the farm; the occasion was a party to celebrate the completion of the lake which Gadie had worked on for three years. Finally it was finished and I had a surprise party for him. Everyone brought gag gifts pertaining to the lake—cork stoppers—rubber ducks—gold fish and so on. I decorated with cattails and gold fish and we had lots of food and lots of champagne.

I want to highlight Hash's presence there because even though it was only four months till she died, nothing in the world would have seemed more absurd than such a thought.

She and James came in and were easily the most stylish couple there. She had on my favorite of all her dresses, the one which now hangs in my closet. It was black and white striped and I had probably suggested that she wear it because so often she would ask me what would look right on certain occasions.

Wearing that dress with the black and white stripes, she accented it with two bracelets, one black and one white and on her "firm and capable" hands she wore several rings. Her hair looked pretty too. Once, long ago, she lamented, "Oh, I wish I could have a pretty shape to my hair like some people do!" At that time her hair was a problem, but in the last ten years or so she was satisfied with her hair because she had found out at last that her hair could "have a shape like other peoples." That was because Ruth started cutting it for her exactly to Hash's desire and she kept it just the way she wanted it. I remember Ruth would drop whatever she was doing and run up whenever Hash asked her to and cut it and give her permanents—she was a great friend, a special friend and Hash depended on her for so much. Once she said she wouldn't trust Ruth with remembering or doing some insignificant thing, but she would "trust her with her life." And indeed she did just that.

Back to the party—she was sparkling that night just like the champagne. She got a kick out of seeing Tom with the cattails and the peacock feathers in his hat and I took several good pictures of her.

Especially did she enjoy the way the house looked as she drove in and she excitedly told me it looked just like "Tara" in "Gone With The Wind." She said the lights coming up the drive and the illuminated lions and especially the chandelier in the hall was so beautiful.

I'm glad she came that night. That was the fourth day of December, then came the bad winter which is dealt with elsewhere, and now I want to recall the way we tried to find out what was wrong with her.

As I related, she was seemingly in perfect health the first of December, then January and February were hard on everyone and we saw her as no exception. But in March it was startlingly obvious that something was wrong with Hash! That whole month is a blur to me and when it was over I couldn't believe it had been a month because it seemed like a week or two.

How wonderful though that if a person must be sick it can be catalogued into a four or five week period as hers was.

I'm not naive enough to say that she was in perfect health and then—wham—a one month illness and that's it. I know now that her condition was developing slowly over the months, but I am saying that she went about her daily life and gave the impression that all was normal. She ate and drank and talked and was Hash—what could go wrong? We thought she was invincible, didn't we?

I would give anything in the world just to get to see her and talk to her and tell her how very much I miss her. Several times, in the early unrealness after her death I would dial 2261, hoping against hope that she would be there and answer. Just to say hello like she had so many hundreds of times before.

Alice, later you told me that you and Mary Ann had done the same thing. Then we found out that Bubble had too.

Several times Gadie has told me that he would give anything he had to see and talk to his mother and grandmother, just for a few minutes. Before, I didn't understand the loneliness and sadness behind such a desire, but now I do. Don't we all?

I have a desire to dream about her like people say you do after awhile. They say your mind will not allow it for some time after they die, but then gradually you will and it is so natural and just as if they were there.

A few nights ago I had a dream like that about Momma. I treasure it. I was down at her house and so happy that I was going to get to sleep with her like I did when I was a little girl. She was standing close to the grate and I went up to her and put my hands on her shoulders and looked at her sweet familiar face. I remember telling her, "Momma, you just don't have any idea how much I love you." It was wonderful because I knew the situation and knew how grateful I was to be allowed this dream and to have Momma there just exactly like she was. I had one dream like that about Hash but it was only her voice over the phone. I couldn't believe it was really her and I asked her where she had been.

So well concealed was her illness that I, and others, knowing something was bothering her, suspected mental worry. Balancing between mental and physical, I opted for mental problems or stress. She, being the very epitome of diligence when it came to meeting attendance, began to show signs that I diagnosed as indifference. Now I realize that with the weakening of her organs and the gradual slowing down of her bodily functions, she was drained of her usual vitality and left at a loss of how to explain it to herself or to us. It was before pain gave it's definite signal—an in-between time when she was not sick but certainly not well. It was in February when these perplexities surfaced and questions arose.

I would call to see if she was ready for me to pick her up for the meeting and she would say she just didn't believe she would be going. Next time she would say she just didn't feel like she had the energy to get dressed.

Once Tracy was there and he told me, with much surprise in his voice, "Hash said she just didn't feel like getting ready for the meeting!"

We were all like the three monkeys who could see no evil, hear no evil and speak no evil. When it came to Hash, we could see no sickness, hear no signs and speak no worry.

She didn't want anyone to worry about her and we certainly didn't want to.

That reminds me of one time when she acted in contrast to her usual "don't worry about me" self. Several years ago, maybe five or six, she had a bad cold. I can't remember her ever having any other illness, can you? She boasted of never ever having a headache in her life. Who else in this world ever got through without having a headache? She was remarkable in her health and for that I am forever grateful.

How she dreaded a cold and would go to great lengths to ward off one. A cold would scare her to death, and she would gargle salt and soda water and take extra vitamin C. She always cautioned us what to do when we felt one coming on.

Anyway, this particular time she uncharacteristically felt sorry for herself for some unknown reason. On the phone she said to me "I don't know why it is but nobody thinks I can ever get sick."

She had always liked Englebert Humperdink. She also liked Dean Martin whom she called "My idea of a man," Billy Thunderkloud and she liked "Little Elvis." Her favorite song by Elvis was "Everlasting Life." I'm so glad that she went to see him with us at his concert at Cincinnati about a year or so before she died. I always wanted her to see him and I had asked her each time I went, but this one time she went and enjoyed it so. I enjoyed it doubly by seeing it through her eyes. She followed Elvis down through the years through me and shared it all: My early silliness as a teenager and then the maturity? that followed. How did she ever stand to hear me play those records over and over? Then she raised the astronomical sum of nine dollars for me to go to Louisville with a group of school friends to see him perform. Then came the day that Virginia Warth stepped off the plane from New York and instead of seeing me come off with her as expected, she was handed a New York newspaper with the glaring headlines: "FANNEE FIELDS ELOPES WITH ELVIS PRESLEY." It was one of those novelty fake newspapers where you can insert your own headlines. I think she even believed it for a minute and then I walked out and shattered her grandiose dreams of mother-in-law glory. Appropriately she was there with me at the farm that August day when Emmy Van Outer phoned with the unbelievable news that Elvis had died. Trying to comfort me, as I was crying so hard, she made what was for her a strange statement. She said: "Don't feel so bad—you still have me." Less than eight months later, I didn't even have her.

So on one February day when I heard that Englebert Humperdink was going to appear in Lexington, I thought it would be nice to take her to see him—maybe it would give her a lift. But here again she "just didn't feel like getting out."

Still wondering whether her lethargy was mental or physical, I remember going to a meeting on Tuesday night that she had declined to attend, and asking Ruth this exact question: "Wonder what's wrong with Hash?" We were genuinely puzzled and highly concerned and we sat and discussed it for twenty minutes or so. I remember that we were more inclined to think something was worrying her rather than to suspect an illness.

Mary Ann, you came in shortly after and I discussed it with you and you decided to take her out to lunch, just the two of you, to try to get her to tell you what was bothering her. I was so anxious for you to return so I could hear the verdict but there was none. She said there was nothing bothering her and I guess there wasn't anything she could put her finger on. She just knew she wasn't quite right, but didn't know why. In fact, something was said to the effect that maybe she didn't feel like doing this or that and Mary Ann, you said she got quite indignant at the thought that she couldn't do everything she always had.

On the same day she ate lunch with you, Mary Ann, you both came over to my house and she held her hand on her shoulder all the time—like it was bothering her, but she seemed unaware that she was doing it. In fact, she had a preoccupied air about her the whole time and a worried look on her face. One incident that stuck in my mind was about the date for our assembly. It had been canceled because of the extremely bad weather. As you were leaving I told her the new date for the assembly, and I was surprised to get no response from her. I supposed she didn't hear me, so I told her again and got only a small response. We looked at one another— worriedly—and shook our heads because of her obvious lack of interest in the assembly which had always sparked her interest like nothing else. Perhaps she was worrying about whether or not she would even feel like going by then...

It was held about three weeks after she died. It was one of the worst experiences I had to go through because so many of her friends came up to me—looking for her. Many of them were from other states and hadn't heard about her. It was so hard to tell them and on one occasion Judy was with me and I had to walk away, leaving her to break the news to one particular friend that Hash held a Bible study with years ago.

Speaking of Judy reminds me of what a tremendous help she has been to me through this whole traumatic ordeal; having experienced the same thing she has had to relive it all through my agony and she has done it unselfishly, as a true friend. One time she was there with me as I cried bitterly, saying: "I just don't think I can stand it." Just having someone to listen in silent sympathy is enough—embellished words are unnecessary.

At this assembly, the speaker mentioned all the troubles that come upon mankind, including death, and then he said, "Aren't we grateful for the wonderful resurrection hope?" Hundreds of people broke into applause and I honestly and truly felt that they were all looking at me and smiling with love.

Going back to the first indications of trouble, I know the very first time it was acknowledged by her to me. We were at the meeting on Sunday. After some hesitation she had decided to go and I picked her up. We had barely sat down when she said she had a pain in her shoulder. I asked her if she wanted to go home and she did. On the way I stopped at Scott County Pharmacy to get some things to relieve her: a hot water bottle, a muscle relaxant and some calcium pills.

On arriving home, I massaged her neck and shoulder muscles. After taking the relaxant and the calcium, she settled on the couch with the hot water bottle and said how good she felt. Little did I know that would be the last meeting she would ever attend.

In fact, jumping ahead now, the thing that made most of us finally realize how serious her illness really was, was when she missed the only occasion we celebrate all year, the Memorial. It was held on March the 23rd.

Knowing now that she did indeed have some physical trouble, and getting an admission from her opened the way for us to begin an almost futile search for help.

Trying to make an appointment with Dr. S., we found it was his day out of the office, but, on hearing that she had abdominal pain he urged us to meet him in the emergency room of the Georgetown Hospital. That we did and the tentative diagnosis was muscle spasms of the stomach. However, he urged us to come into his office several days later for a more extensive examination and X-Rays. That we did and I can remember seeing her on that table looking up so worriedly as he examined her. He was worried too.

The X-Rays were taken and sent to be read and we waited in the office. Hepatitis was mentioned as a possibility—the liver evidently showed trouble to the doctor as it was obviously enlarged. The X-Rays came back and were read—gallstones—one large one and several small ones.

This diagnosis in no way alarmed me—in fact I was relieved. When I gave the news later to some of her friends who were anxiously awaiting the announcement, I presented it in that way and they said my face was all lit up and I said "Hash has gallstones!" You do understand that I was relieved because in lieu of all the other things I knew it could be, that was a relief.

Surprisingly though, Hash didn't regard gallstones as lightly as I did. She seemed so worried and I sincerely told her that as far as I was concerned gallstones were a minor worry and I had heard of dozens of people who had them. Her reply was, in retrospect, prophetic and chilling—"Yes, and I know some people they have put under too."

We were sent to the hospital kitchen to get a special menu for her to follow for two weeks with the hope that they would be gotten under control without the necessity of an operation which she even seemed to dread the thought of.

At the time, the GALLSTONES loomed all important and we focused on them, but looking back, after the whole picture was completed, we can see that they were only the tip of the iceberg and served only as a warning signal to lead us into the real and serious trouble lurking there.

We gave the two weeks time only two or three days. My intuition told me that it wasn't working and that time was not to be wasted—not even one hour of it. How glad I am that we tried. How desperately we tried...

Next we decided to use the olive oil and juice treatment to dissolve them as at least four people that I know had done and it *had* positively worked for them. It's a natural method and it does have results and she did indeed pass many, many, bile green crystals.

How elated we were—how jubilant! Now she would start getting better! Her body, which all these years had been so magnificent in it's vibrant health would respond in it's awesome way and everything would be alright. Hadn't she always told us so—couldn't we believe it still?

No, we couldn't, because under our close scrutiny there was no sign of improvement.

How desperately I waited each morning to hear some spark in her voice when I called her. How I questioned her: "Did you sleep?" and "Do you have any appetite this morning?"—"Do you feel any better at all?"

I would hurry up each day and take any nourishing or appetizing thing I could possibly think of to try to get some food or drink into her. I knew she must eat—but she couldn't.

Recently I read an article in the paper reporting that an alarming number of people with certain illnesses die from malnutrition or simple starvation than they do from the illness itself. I believe that to be true in her case. Her body just couldn't digest the food, plus the fact that she had absolutely no desire for it either, therefore there was nothing whatsoever for her to fight infection and disease with.

Whether or not that was her case, it is just as well that she didn't have the energy to fight, because the fight would have been for just a little while, considering the enemy's strong hold.

Honey, strawberries and bananas were concoctions I whipped up in my blender to tempt her appetite, but to no avail. She would take several tiny sips through the straw and brag on how delicious it was. I would watch her, but she could never take anymore. It's a good thing she didn't force it because her body just wouldn't accept it—not anymore.

The next step in our quest was to Dr. M—a naturepath in Lexington.

Dr. S. had been called again and he had suggested setting her up for a sounding of her abdomen in Lexington—but for after Easter—and again I felt we couldn't wait.

Dr. M. found that there was trouble in her liver and I reasoned that all the radium treatments she had been subjected to three years earlier had weakened her organs to such an extent that they couldn't respond as they normally would have.

I remember Ruth and Hash and me sitting at the long table in his waiting room and I made out a list of things she needed to talk to him about. You know how scattered she could get and so completely off the subject. She was notorious for that, wasn't she?

She looked so sick and weak when we left there and I helped her to the car because she was so unsteady. My mother was never unsteady before and I couldn't quite believe it.

The next day or so we decided to go to a doctor she had been to before and liked so well—a specialist named Dr. G in Lexington.

She wasn't too weak at this time and seemed quite normal as she dressed and fixed her face and hair. I ran back in the house to get a pillow to prop her up a little—to make her more comfortable. She didn't even mind the ride and we didn't have to wait too long in the office.

Dr. G. examined her abdomen and I could see such worry on his concerned face. A chill went through me as he told us that "There is trouble in there." He sat at his desk and talked to the three of us and didn't try to paint a rosy picture. I desperately wanted him to smile and dispel the dreaded feeling of what was next—to wave his hand and let everything be alright.

She wanted to know if he thought it was a recurrence of the malignant tumor of three years ago—he couldn't say for sure until there were tests made.

She said she would "rather die than go through that again," referring to the treatment of the earlier tumor. He said, "Well, in all honesty Mrs. Jones, you very likely wouldn't be here today if you hadn't gone through that treatment."

She meekly admitted that he was right and that perhaps it wasn't all that bad.

The next step was to the Medical Center the following day for tests set up by Dr. G.

This whole episode at the emergency room I consider more or less an insult to our intelligence as I look back at it. I realize that we were grasping for anything to brighten the outlook and to give us hope, but this was ridiculous.

James and I stayed in the emergency room waiting area while she was taken into a small room to be examined.

After forty-five minutes we were told by the person who did the examining that as far as he could tell there was nothing wrong with any of her vital organs whatsoever, and that the only trouble must be in the gallbladder. He urged us to have X-Rays done immediately on the gallbladder. We said we would do so the next day as it was too late by then for him to do them that day.

Can you imagine our joy and relief—no trouble in any other area! Just a gallbladder problem! How we rejoiced and I called everyone that was anxiously awaiting the news.

When I called Ruth, she told me to tell Hash, who was lying on the couch, that this was the best news she had ever heard—in all her life!

Even Hash accepted it, it seemed. She let down her pretenses and expressed to us, for the very first time, her concern.

So she clutched at the same elusive straw of hope that we did and she revealed the fear she had been living with. But it was not to be—the hope was short-lived. But how it sustained and lifted us there momentarily.

A thought just this moment came to me and I never consciously formed this thought before: We found out differently but she never actually did! Wouldn't it be wonderful if she carried the "all organs are sound" thought with her all the time she was in the hospital? Even though we pursued this thing and ended up hearing the terrible verdict, she never did hear it! How I hope she clung to the gallstone idea and expected it at any time to clear up.

While on the subject, I want to point out one more little thing that happened as we came home that day. I had her arm and was helping her to the porch when suddenly her legs just seemed to melt beneath her. She went down on one knee because she was so weak and my mind rebelled and fought against such a thing...I see her running with Scarlett, laughing as she swings her around and lifts her up to carry her, even though her legs are as long as a young colt...Hash, the agile, limber mother we knew, the mother who prided herself on her agility, should not fall. Unbelievably, she even made some laughing excuse for it but she was short of breath by the time we got to the couch.

Before I go any further, I want to emphasize the point that we were not told that she was alright and all was well. It's just that we were expecting such bad news and just because it was put off for another day and we were momentarily reassured it didn't mean it wasn't there.

If I had been using my head and not my heart I could have easily realized then, as I did later, that no X-Rays were taken, no blood samples were taken and nothing explicit was done except an outward examination which involved probing and feeling and looking.

As he said, *to all outward appearances*, all was in order. But the tests and X-Rays tell the story and that was to come later. We should not have been so gullible. So what I am saying is that if you have "extensive" testing done by a doctor and he says you are alright, then believe him. Don't let this incident make you distrust the diagnosis, because it was definitely not a diagnosis—only an opinion, but we embraced it with open hearts.

The next day was a frantic blur of frustration and telephone calls. Trying to set up an appointment for an X-Ray would seem relatively easy, but I won't even try to go into the delays and problems James and I encountered. We called every place, but to no avail. We could not, believe it or not, even contact the intern who advised the X-Rays even though we tried repeatedly all morning. In desperation we even tried to get an X-Ray at the chiropractor's office here in town, but his machine was broken down. Then we decided that a chiropractor in Lexington—a Dr. G., might be able to see her and take an X-Ray. We called him and he waited in his office for almost an hour for us to get here.

Here begins one of the worst experiences of the whole ordeal. It was because she was by now in the worst stage of her illness so far and it was painful to see her distress.

Slowly and with great effort she dressed to go. I held her clothes while she stepped into them and I put her shoes on her and combed her hair.

They gave us wrong directions and it took several stops and starts to find the right building and even then the three of us had to walk over a block. That was torture for her but we didn't realize how much because she tried to minimize it. After going up several floors to his office, she had to undress and be subjected to a painful treatment and still no X-Ray.

By now I was leading her from the table to the chair and putting her blouse back on her like a child. She was no longer in control. She would have fallen from the table if I hadn't balanced her when it was angled to step down from. It was a nightmare.

She would scream "you're killing me" when Dr. G. pressed on her back with too much force. I felt like I was dying too—my mind screamed for him to stop.

On his face I could see an expression that was hard to comprehend, and not until months later could I make any sense of it. At the time I felt that maybe he had no compassion or sympathy and was in a hurry to get away; that was in contrast to the picture many other people had of him—people who had known him for many years.

When I read in the paper that he too had died, six months later, from cancer of the stomach, I could understand something. He must have seen himself in Hash's symptoms and it must have terrified him. That was the thing I saw in his face—a glimpse of his destiny—and it caused him great distress. This is only my simple theory.

James went to get the car and she and I sat on the sidewalk bench to wait. The wind was cold and whipping around the building and she kept a scarf pulled up around her face and neck. It seemed to take forever for James to get the car and get back to us. She was so miserable and all she wanted was to get back home to lie down.

At home, friends came in and out and called to see about her, but she was gradually fading, losing touch with reality. When I would have to leave to go home for something, I would have Scarlett stay there to answer the phone. Hash got to the point where she slept all the time on the couch and didn't even hear the incessant ringing of the phone. We would be talking to her and in the middle of a sentence she would fall asleep. Those of us who were there would look at one another incredulously—how could such a thing be? Hash was always the epitome of alertness but now the merciful sleep was in control of her.

Now to the last step of our quest for help—an appointment with another specialist—Dr. F.

It was the following day after seeing Dr. G. that I called the very busy Dr. F. and amazingly got an appointment for that very day! It was unheard of and how we appreciated it. I packed her bag, hoping desperately that he would admit her to the hospital, and Alice and I got her to the car. I don't remember how she felt in the car, but the day before as we drove up she commented on how she felt. She said "as long as I sit here without moving, I feel just wonderful."

This day we had a hard time finding a place to park, but finally got in the lot behind the office. There was only a short space to walk from the car to the door and I ran on ahead to tell the receptionist that we were there because we were late.

Alice walked slowly on, holding Hash's arm. Then such a sad thing happened. She fell again. Just a minor fall—barely a skinned knee—but just to think about it even now tears my heart out...Sometimes I would call her and she would be laughing when she answered; I knew she had been leaping through the air again as she ran to answer the phone. She would tell me how hilarious she must have looked, leaping and twirling through the air, sometimes naked as she ran from the tub. Lively, rambuncious movements made her giddy and happy and how agile she had been—just months ago...she was so courageous and kept pushing on, yet so weak she could barely stand. When she fell to her knees something very important inside of me crumbled too. To this day Alice, you and I cannot discuss it, can we, because it was far too traumatic. But these are the very things I must probe back into now, to pull them from the darkened corners of my mind where I have pushed them, because if not, they will always be there, causing pain.

Dr. F. was an extremely kind, compassionate man who gave the impression that he truly cared. In fact, I sent him a card after the funeral, thanking him for that warm concern.

He lost no time in examining her and I could tell that he saw trouble immediately. As I had done at each examination, I stood beside her as she lay on the table to be of whatever comfort or assistance I could.

This time she made some feeble attempt at a joke as she said to me, "Look at her, she won't look on her mother's nakedness." This was in reference to Noah's two sons who looked at their father as he lay drunk and naked and for which they were cursed.

I always respected her modesty, even in this condition and she was still alert enough to take note of it and kid me about it.

Dr. F. needed no added tests or X-Rays to see that she was seriously ill. As his worried eyes met mine as we stood on opposite sides of her, he said the words I had been begging for the last two or three weeks—"I'm going to admit her to the hospital." I nodded in mute agreement.

It took us through three hospitals, two emergency rooms, one doctor, one chiropractor, one naturepath and two specialists before we attained some definite word on her condition.

Thus culminated our originally concerned, but finally frantic, quest for help.

# 10
# I WATCHED YOU LEAVE

Getting into the hospital was even a hassle as there was no available room that day.

The following day, James and I called the hospital and doctor's office hourly, as we had been asked to do, to find out immediately when a room was available.

Hash was by now completely isolated from the whole procedure and felt none of the anxiety her many friends and family felt. She slept on the couch, aided by the merciful pain pills at intervals.

At last, in the late afternoon, the blessed news came that a room was ready for her at Good Samaritan Hospital.

Even now, I still get a certain sick feeling when I remember back to those traumatic ten days she was in there. It all rushes back—the sickening worry, the unspoken questions in everyone's eyes and most of all, the fear that clutched at us constantly.

What a relief it was to have her settled in the room, knowing that at last she would have the help she needed. It was Thursday, March 30.

Alice and James both planned to stay with her that night, but I insisted that I stay, so Alice went to work at about seven that evening and James went home after visiting hours.

I pulled two chairs together and slept at times, but mostly I watched her and listened to her labored breathing. I couldn't understand at the time why she breathed in such short breaths, but much later, when I learned about her lungs, I understood.

I'm so glad I stayed with her and was there to help her. She was not even conscious enough to have called a nurse and to have rung a bell. I would see her starting to get up to go to the bathroom and I would help her to the door.

Once there, she each time during the night insisted that I go back and leave her in there alone, saying she was alright. This insisting was done however with a weak wave of her hand and a minimum of words—"go on back."

Morning came and with it the request for blood samples and urine specimens. There was no food or drink for her and even if there had been, she couldn't have taken it.

Here again I have to relate one of the painful episodes she and I encountered; facing the grim reality of her now limited capabilities and my forced acceptance of it.

On one occasion she had to bend down to the floor and when she tried to get up, she couldn't.

It was almost more than my mind could comprehend. Here was Hash, the nimble mother of my youth, who could outdo everyone else around when it came to any graceful movement—not able to rise from her position on the floor.

I grasped her in whatever way I could and with a momenteous effort she got up, only to fall almost lifeless sideways on the bed, too weak to get on it right.

Being too short of breath to utter a full sentence all morning made what she said next all the more touching: "Did you ever think you'd see your mother too weak to get up by herself?" Those were the last words I heard from her for quite awhile.

The aid came then to take her down for X-Rays in a wheel chair. Seeing that she was unable to get off the bed and seeing my distress, he mercifully came back with a rolling bed to take her on. How I appreciated that—to let her lie on a bed rather than to sit up in a chair.

Then began a series of X-Rays downstairs of which she was completely unaware. She just slipped away from me on the way down in the elevator. She didn't appear to be asleep—it was more like a semi-coma.

I stood beside her all the time and spoke occasionally but she never answered or responded in any way. She was completely still and quite and unaware of any of the tests.

I had to step out of the room as they took the actual X-Rays, but they would call me back in when they finished each one and still no response.

Finally they finished and we were on our way back to the elevator. Then we met you, Mary Ann. You had hurried in from Ashland to be there early—the first of many such trips you made in the next eight days. You and little Tiffany, only three months old and so unbelievably good through it all.

You looked at her and I can still see your stricken face as you uttered the prophetic words, "she's dying".....

Later, in analyzing our reactions to her condition, Mary Ann, you more or less pinpointed our whole outlook on life.

I immediately denied your above statement there by the elevator, more or less chiding you for such words. "Ridiculous," I said, "she is just sick and weak. She'll be alright as soon as they start treating her."

That was me—always expecting things to be alright; not only expecting it, but indeed believing it whole-heartedly that they *would* be alright.

Then there was your attitude, Alice. Later you said you knew all along she was going to die, but you wouldn't admit it, to anyone, especially to yourself. Such thoughts are not to be tolerated but to be pushed back into the far recesses of the mind. So you pretended she would be alright while I knew she would.

But you, Mary Ann, with your dark, pessimistic thoughts, was the smartest one of all. You knew how bad it was at that first tortured glance and you were honest enough with yourself to face it and not gloss over what you knew to be true. Expecting the worst didn't make it any easier when it came though, did it?

My optimistic side notwithstanding, I was siezed with a feeling of panic when we reached the room and Hash was again settled in the bed, showing no response whatsoever.

Mary Ann, your keen observation must have moved me whether my mind registered it as true or not. I put aside whatever meekness I might be noted for and had the audacity, spurred on by desperation, to get the eminient specialist Dr. F. on the phone and tell him he "had to do something!"

I'm sure he had an office full of patients and was very busy, but in his characteristically kind way, he merely said "I'll be right there" and he was.

I remember telling him on the phone that here it was the second day and nothing whatsoever had been done for her—no intravenous feeding or medication—nothing but tests.

Realizing later that they couldn't treat her until the important tests revealed what was to be treated, I understood the situation better, but at the time I only knew I wanted some action. I wanted to see her conscious and alert—I wanted her to be Hash again. But it was not to be.

There was a quick flurry of activity in the next forty-five minutes or so after Dr. F. arrived. The X-Rays were brought to him and I could feel and hear the seriousness of the situation as he and his associate Dr. M. hastily conferred on her case.

As they strode down the hall, hurriedly, as is the way with doctors, I ran along beside them, practically unobserved, and listened with my heart.

One statement that caught my ears both relieved and frightened me simultaneously, if such a thing can be. The words were, "I think you'll agree with me that she should be put in the intensive care unit right away."

Dr. F. hurried off to make the necessary arrangements and I cornered Dr. M. with some questions. He explained that there was obvious trouble in the abdomen, possibly involving the kidneys and the pancreas.

I called James at work and he came immediately. He was planning to come anyway right after an important meeting they were having but never expecting such drastic steps. Neither were we.

Alice, you and I hovered outside the door where they had taken her and finally you had the boldness to push open the forbidden door and look in. What you saw made you turn pale and I barely got you to a cot in the hall. Later you told me you saw them putting the tubes in her nose and mouth and it startled you so.

Now it was starkly official—Hash was seriously ill. The repercussions were felt all around and phones rang constantly; anxious friends and relatives seeking news of her condition and almost willing her improvement. She was blessed with an abundance of friends who genuinely loved her. One such friend, who is about my age, told me with no guilt whatsoever that it was much harder on her than if it had been her own mother. That's the way many people felt about her—they felt she belonged to them, in a way. She was "family." This same girl said when she thought of Hash she always thought of her smiling. She always had that smile for you—always. Not a sweet smile necessarily, but more of an impish, alert smile.

Lowell, I'll always be thankful, as I'm sure you will be too, that your intuition made you call from  Florida to "see how Hash was."

That was an unprecedented move on your part and how tragic it would have been otherwise. You travel around to parts unknown quite often and keeping your whereabouts quiet is your style and your right.

But this time your obscurity would have prevented us from contacting you with the news of her sickness and even her death. What a tragic shock to come home to.

To my great relief you called me early Saturday morning from some part of Florida. I had come home the night before and was ready to hurry back up when you called.

Knowing how excitable you can get, I tried to break the intensive care news to you in an easy way. I heard you say "I'm leaving right now" and my reply of "Don't drive wild" fell on the dial tone...

That was about eight o'clock in the morning and to my amazement you were there at three or four o'clock the next morning. I was asleep in a chair in the little waiting room where all the tortured souls try to rest and you walked in, having already been up to look at her, breaking the rules, as usual.

That Saturday and Sunday was a blur of emotions: dreadful anxiety, disbelief, bright moments of hope, numbing fear, optimism, unanswerable questions and unacceptable facts.

But through it all we were there, glued together by our fear. How we searched the face of one who had been to see her first or the one to whom the doctor had spoken.

Even now, I can still feel the bottomless feeling in my stomach and the numbness of my whole being as we filed into her cubicle like room in intensive care at the two hour intervals. Walking in with a certain dreadful eagerness, at times we would find her lying inert and unresponsive, but at other times she would meet our eyes with a remote smile of recognition.

Those are the moments we would grasp and cling to and repeat them over and over to all who asked about her—how we hoped it meant she was improving! And then we would hurry out so other loved ones could have their measured moments with her in the desperate ten minutes we were alloted. That was the worst part of all—leaving her room. I would always back out, reluctant to turn my back, knowing that the precious last glance would possibly be the last...

How heart-rending even now to relive, the trying to memorize every feature and prolong an instant in time—attempting to immortalize her in my mind. It's vague and blurry in my mind now, as it was then, just exactly what all happened.

At intervals on Saturday and Sunday she was talking and conscious and the thing that was remarkable was that she had not only some comment to make to all who made the sad trek to her bedside, but a comment that pertained to them personally. She was aware and alert in a fuzzy sort of way and we analyzed every word she uttered, didn't we?

As she was lying there, obviously thinking of something, Mary Ann, you asked her what she was thinking about and she replied: "I was just thinking about how lifeless I feel."

Then you asked her, "You do want to get well, don't you?" You said she dismissed such a negative thought with a quick assurance that she did.

We brushed her hair, and Alice, you did her eyebrows. She always used to say she would rather be seen naked than without her eyebrows, so you always made sure they were just right. She used to "curse" me for having taken all her eyebrows since I have such bushy ones. It seems as if she said the same thing about Uncle Pal, though I can't imagine why.

When Sharon went in for a quick visit one time, we didn't think she was quite aware of her surroundings, but she quickly dispelled that thought when she made some comment on the cute upturned nose of Sharon's little girl, Autumn.

She also said, "I never saw so many good loyal people" in reference to all her friends there.

Once when I walked in by myself she looked up and sweetly said, "There's my sunshine."

Once, in a show of improvement, she even raised her body up off the bed with her heels and elbows, all the while tossing us a triumphant look. We rejoiced with her, remembering how she had been unable to move freely for weeks.

Uncle Pal kidded her about having so many visitors, saying she should charge admission and as he walked out of the room she retorted: "a quarter." With him, she also laughed over a religious joke they had shared before. She always loved "Henry."

Scarlett and Tracy were slipped in to her bedside, standing straight and white and in dreadful awe of the wires and tubes and machines and the unreality of it all.

How I resented the machine that told her "life story" and even though I resented and hated it, I watched it constantly. The numbers of her pulse and heartbeat or whatever were there for all to see—speeding up and slowing down—and I realized it was beating out a rhythm of life or death that I was powerless to change.

Tubes were taking fluid out of her body and other carried strength into it. She, who always despised such things, voiced no complaint that I know of. She took it all uncomplainingly except for one point she was adamant on—she wanted water!

We would put Blistex on her parched mouth and hold a wet washcloth to her lips, but it didn't help much; nothing does when you are craving water.

The nurse let her brush her teeth one time and rinse with a mouthful of water because she said she wouldn't swallow any of it. Billy, how you laughed when you told later about seeing one little quick sip of water sneak through the tube, belying her words.

Then, Mary, you and Alice hit upon the idea of chewing gum and to our delight, the nurse gave her permission. Mary Ann, I remember you flying downstairs to get some and being back in record time. You presented it to her and it was utterly delightful—one bright spot in the whole ordeal—seeing her chew on it as if it were golden nectar.

Like a pack rat she snatched the package from you as you started to take it to leave with the nurse, and hid it beneath her mattress. Black eyes flashing, she snapped: "She won't get that."

As we walked out that time we were laughing and I can still see her through the window—propped up and chomping away and faintly waving her hand.

But there were the other times—the ones I can hardly bear to remember. They are the ones I must force myself to relive and to tell and in doing so I may free myself of pent-up feelings of pain. That is one of the purposes of the book, if you recall, to bring out into the light the painful memories as well as the happy ones.

I loved her all my life, as we all did, with a carefree, easy love, appreciative and secure in our relationship. With her I also shared a great rapport and innumerable times we would start to say the exact thing or react to a situation in the same way. Even now, I can hear a remark or song or see something that evokes a reaction that I know would be the same as hers. You might say we were kindred spirits, and I'm sure several of you might have felt the same about yourself.

I sincerely appreciated her and we enjoyed doing things together and I had a good warm feeling toward her—a proud feeling.

Yes, I loved her with all my heart and I know without any doubt she knew it, but...I never *told* her that I loved her.

When she was in the intensive care unit I was expecting every moment to be the last and I begged the nurses to let us be with her when the end came. More than anything in the world, I didn't want her to die alone.

When the nurses has us leave after one ten-minute visit, I truly thought she would be gone before the next visit. She was unconscious and so still, and I just felt so sure the end was near. So I slipped back in and sat on my knees on the floor so they couldn't see me through the window.

I told her over and over how much I loved her but she couldn't hear me then.

If you love someone, don't just take it for granted but be sure to tell them while you can, while they can still hear you...

Once, in the throes of our sadness, while awaiting her fate, I was asked by you, Lowell, as to where my faith was. You wondered why I didn't have faith that she would get well.

It was because I know that, as Ecclesiastes says, time and circumstance befall us all, and Jehovah God doesn't promise to prolong our lives miraculously now, but he does promise to remember his good servants by means of a resurrection in the future. So I was willing to accept whatever might come, having full assurance that she would receive His smile of approval. Therefore I could accept her imminent death, putting it in the right perspective, and not feeling the outcome as an acceptance or a rejection of my prayers.

I know, as did she, that death is indeed a great enemy, but one that at times, might, in complete contradiction even be called a friend. I look at her case as an example of this.

Hash accepted this same promise from the Bible and years before, when she had her other trouble, I know that she had prayed, not for miraculous healing, but for the strength to accept whatever might come and to be remembered at the end.

That Saturday while I was somewhere in the hospital I heard Dr. F. paged and I ran as fast as I could up the stairs to her room just in time to see him dash past me into her room. She had evidently been in such sudden desperate pain that he was called to administer a block, the first one of several. It cut off the pain to her organs and gave her blessed relief and sleep.

Then came that terrible Sunday that I will always remember. We were all there, in varying stages of grief and hope, keeping a vigil. Dr. F.'s associate came to the coffee shop where most of you were sitting at the long table and broke the sad news—"it does look like she is dying."

I was elsewhere at the time and Gadie came after me with such a sadness on his face. You can tell so much from a face that words are not always necessary.

There in the hall and through the lobby was a sight that even now fills me with emotion. It had been announced at the meeting that Sunday at the Kingdom Hall that her condition had worsened and a terrible sadness had drawn her loyal friends to come to where she was to give us their silent support and comfort.

The sadness was overwhelming and words were unnecessary as I looked at all of them and saw my grief reflected repeatedly in their good faces. The imminent loss of a person who had been so very special to them was felt there in the hallway.

When I went in to see her after that she was conscious and I told her how her sweet friends were downstairs, knowing of course that they couldn't come up, and she smiled and said how good it was of them to come. I told her that someone thought we were having a convention because there were so many people.

Somehow that day finally ended and then the night was to be reckoned with. Alice and James stayed and Sharon, the loyal friend, did too. I slept out front in James' car, expecting to be called in at any moment, but with the morning light came the wonderful realization that she was still alive—she had made it through the night.

For that I am so grateful—the fact that she lived six more days. It gave us a chance to reconcile ourself to the fact that death was more than a probability, even though we still clung tenaciously to hope, and to be better prepared for it when it came. I'm so thankful that we and she had those next six days because she was moved from intensive care to a normal room on Monday or Tuesday and the atmosphere was so much different than the sterile world of the intensive care unit.

Here we were allowed to believe that maybe, just maybe, things would be alright again and our world would once again be bright. The flowers that Billy chose from the florist across the street and the ones James brought, combined with the offer and acceptance by her of a rental TV, seemed to restore some degree of normalcy to the nightmare of the preceding days.

Now she was even able to drink any time she desired and how she appreciated that even though she grimaced every time the water hit her throat. How we delighted to see her off the monitoring machine and the tubes taken from her nose; now I honestly believed that maybe it was a massive infection in her body set up by gallstones or whatever.

Doctors and all their modern techniques could easily deal with an infection and how desperately I hoped that was the problem—I sincerely didn't think by then that it was anything any more serious.

Oh, how we analyzed every detail available to us, clinging to each medical term dropping from the doctor's lips, questioning the interns and the aids for their opinion and turning over and over each shred of information we could gather—desperate for a scrap of hope.

Dr. F. leaned toward the massive infection idea; Dr. M. toward a suspected tumor. Dr. F. more or less hinted that Dr. M. was pressing for a biopsy and while he didn't say so, I felt that he was stalling. Perhaps he knew what would follow the biopsy and was just giving us a little more time........

Through it all, the one who made the days more bearable and in this case, took us away from reality, was Uncle Pal, known in other circles as Henry Robertson. He was there all the time, and made the whole ordeal much lighter with his jokes and banter. He made us feel that things just weren't that bad, and in some way, that even if they were, life would still go on.

He was in and out all day, and would whisk us out for lunch, giving us a much—needed break. It must have been heart-rending for him to look in on her as he did each time, to remember when she had always had a quick retort to his witty remarks and matched him verse for verse in their oft-quoted favorite poems. The partially concealed pain in his eyes and his hasty exits revealed what his casual demeanor belied—he too was grief-stricken.

I'll always appreciate his support at that time and the good feeling I had just seeing him there. It was the same as when I was a little girl; then he made life seem several shades brighter with his jokes and teasing. Because of that, Lowell, you bestowed upon him the name that signified what he was to all of us kids—our Uncle "Pal."

For the next four days she fluctuated between semi-consciousness and awareness; our hopes being lifted or dashed accordingly. Food was brought one day and I excitedly offered her a spoonful, only to have her decline it before she slipped back into her dark sleep.

Looking back, I truly feel she used to it's fullest extent her ability to completely relax and block out the unwelcome reality. I doubt very much that any of you have any comprehension of what I mean. It's a unique ability of being able to rise above the threshold of pain to a great extent. There is nothing mystical whatsoever about it and it is nothing that she and I ever discussed.

Anytime I have been in pain, such as at childbirth, I have relaxed so completely that it was as if I rose above my body and let the pain sweep through an empty shell. I really had the feeling of floating on top of myself, aware each time of when to release my muscles before the next pain came. Therefore my childbearing was amazingly swift and quite easy.

Trying to teach this method, Alice, to you and Mary Ann, I realized the futility of it because complete relaxation to such a point was impossible for the two of you to accomplish.

Frankly, I would suppose there are very few people who are that relaxed, but I believe Hash was.

Even when I do hard exercises, such as sit-ups, I find myself closing my eyes and disassociating myself from the ordeal.

The classic example to prove my point took place on the examining table of my gynecologist, Dr. Preston. As all of us of the female gender know, we tend to become quite tense at the prospect of such an examination. He was delayed and the nurse stuck her head in to tell me it would be a few mintues before he could get to me. Putting my relaxation bit into practice, I apparently over-did it—falling asleep on that stiff table on my back with nothing but a sheet clutched to me! It worked! Repeating my surety that this is nothing mystical whatsoever, but just the ability to disassociate myself from my surroundings at times, reminds me of one occasion when I was about ten or twelve years old. It was in the front yard of the church at Muddy Ford, apparently after a revival at night. Everyone was out front talking and mingling in groups and I said to Hash, "I feel like I'm looking down on all this." She quickly told me to hush and looked nervously around to see if anyone had overheard me. What a strange child! I haven't even thought if that in years.

But as you all know I am strange and my mind is quite often miles away from where it should be. I have been labeled a daydreamer and accused of living in a dream world and I don't deny any of it. At times, I may be looking you right in the eye, supposedly attentive, but that doesn't mean that I am. I might just be flying along on the wings of my mind to a place of long ago and far away.........It's just the way I am, and it has helped me a lot........although it hasn't made this ordeal of her death one bit easier.

So without a doubt, I honestly feel that she chose to drift along in the inbetween world of sleep rather than face the reality of pain. I believe she must have known what was waiting for her and chose to surrender rather than to fight a losing battle, a painful battle.

One reason I feel she looked at sleep as a friend is because of some very dramatic words she directed at me the day before she died: "Don't let them wake me up again!" I wanted to shout at her the lines from the Dylan Thomas poem:

"Do not go gentle into that good night.......
Rage, rage against the dying of the light."

I didn't want her to drift away from us so softly—I didn't want her to leave in any way........

I also remember hurrying one morning to get to the hospital and hearing Elvis sing on the radio that sad, sad song, "Softly, as I leave you........Long before your arms can beg me stay, for one more hour, for one more day........"

So our vigil continued; Alice sleeping all night on the chair and going in to check on her as often as allowed and Mary Ann coming back and forth with little Tiffany as if it was no problem at all. James there throughout—engulfed in a haze of worry but at times allowing his hopes to rise dangerously high. Billy and Lowell were in and out at every chance, sitting by her bed and being there till eleven or twelve at night in the stiff waiting room. Friends coming and going, unable to see her but giving comfort by their presence, and the incessant ring of the phone in the waiting room— "how is she?"

Little Tiffany was only three months old and unbelievably good. Soon she was known all over the hospital and people gravitated to her as to a ray of sunshine in this cold, sad place. This was at times to Mary Ann's dismay, I might add, as she visualized the myriads of germs transferred to Tiffany by the stranger's hands.

At this time, Mary Ann, you were still in that emotionally shaky ground which mothers of new babies are so familiar with. How you ever held up, I'll never know, but somehow you did, all the while giving the impression that all was well with you. In fact, you constantly worried about my well-being until one time I said, "My goodness, you are the one you should be worried about!"

Then came one beautiful shining day that gave her back to us, but for only a short precious while. It is all the more poignant when you realize why she appeared to be so much improved. We decided later, Mary and I, that her valiant good body which had served her so faithfully all these years must have made one last momentous effort before it failed. It rallied above and beyond the call of duty—imparting the color of life to her face and a spark to her dark eyes—letting us catch one last precious glimpse of her as we remembered her.

I have heard it explained medically that the body does often do that. Haven't you heard it said that a sick person often shows a great surge of improvement just before the worst part comes?

Dr. F. came in to check her and in all sincerity he exclaimed, "You've already got your drug store face on!" He really believed she had makeup on; her skin looked that much better! Alice fixed her eyebrows and we brushed her hair and she smiled so sweetly as we clustered around her in happiness.

That must have been Thursday. People came and went; some went in but others didn't want to disturb her. Jimmy came after work every night—anxious to hear of any progress and so full of concern.

That night Gadie came and when he went into the room she said "There's that handsome man." She always thought so much of Gadie; when we were the first ones married, before Mary and Alice, she would call Gadie "her favorite son-in-law!" Such tact!

This night Gadie was telling her a dream he had about her the night before. He got such a good response from her, and so pleased was he to make her laugh, he went through the whole thing again. I can see exactly how she laughed—with her mouth closed and just shaking her head sideways. It wasn't her regular laugh, but it pleased us to see any kind of reaction. She reminded me so much of Momma when she did that.

David Robertson came in to see her too. She, being his Aunt and he, being a doctor, naturally meant we couldn't wait to get an unofficial diagnosis from him.

After looking at her, he remarked that she did indeed look sick, but he didn't think she looked, as we all agreed, "dying sick"........She would have been proud, had she known, of the performance her faithful body played that day, conjuring up a picture of health and improvement when in actuality it was it's final deceit.

The following day, the intern in charge of her insisted that we must stay out and give her more rest; she wasn't getting the relief she should from the pain killers he was administering to her. He was trying everything available to find one that was effective and strong enough, and our presence was more or less keeping her in an agitated state. He advised us not to go in the room so she would not be interrupted, therefore giving the medication time to work.

We did as he asked, except to look in at intervals. Once I jumped up and ran into the room, thinking I heard her call my name but she was asleep and I must have been mistaken.......

After peeping around the door and seeing her supposedly asleep, James, Alice and I and maybe Mary,decided to go home for a few hours.

At home there were many pressing things that called out to me: clothes to be washed, some short time to be spent with Scarlett and Tracy, a nourishing supper to be cooked for a change. Good friends had brought in food for them while I was gone, but still I needed to cook and eat a meal with them too.

My mind reasoned that I should go home but I felt such a heaviness, as if I was making the wrong decision. This was the first time she was left alone, as far as I remember, and my steps slowed as we got to the elevator, to the front door, and on the way to the car, but still I reasoned that a few hours wouldn't really matter, since she was doing so well and we had been advised to let her rest.

I remember standing by the car and looking way up at that window in the waiting room. I remember how happy and confident James was that she was going to be alright. I remember thinking that Scarlett and Tracy needed me for a few hours. Against my better judgment I got into the car and left. I'll always regret it.

This is another of the painful memories I must relive, and in so doing make it more bearable to myself. In relating it now, my stomach gets upset and my head feels dizzy and I feel a compulsion to scream or something.

We were back in about three or four hours. Hurrying into her room and finding her asleep, I questioned the lady who shared the room with her as to how she did while we were gone. Her reply: "That poor woman suffered death all afternoon. I never felt so sorry for anyone in my life. She called over and over for someone to just come and hold her hand." Against my will I asked, almost inaudibly, "who did she call for?" She answered: "I didn't catch all the names, but I heard her call for James........and for Fannee........"

After reliving the agony I must also share with you the relief that it was the only time she suffered so desperately. That is the merciful part—it didn't go on and on. I think about people, like Shelia Bramlett who had to live through that experience numerous times with people they loved. I feel unspeakable sorrow for them and immense relief and gratefulness for the swiftness of my mother's illness. For that I am so thankful—that she didn't linger on in pain.

Then came Saturday—April the eighth—1978. This was the day she died. I'm so glad she died in the spring. Somehow that made it more bearable. Like the words in the song she loved—"Honey." "It was in the early spring, when flowers bloomed and robins sing, she went away........"

She loved April. When she was a young girl, a long time ago, she planned to have a little girl and name her April. I don't know why Mary Ann, Fannee and Alice replaced April, but they did.

Saturday morning we were still asked to stay out of the room as much as possible. She appeared to be resting more, except occasionally she would toss around and moan.

Lunch time came and I encouraged the others who were there to go on down and eat and I would stay till they came back, then take my turn.

Slipping quietly into her room, I sat in the chair at the side of her bed, not making a sound. Soon another person entered the room and after watching her closely, he silently motioned me to follow him out. It was Dr.

M. Feeling a dread I didn't really understand, I asked him: "Are you going to do the biopsy?" He nodded his head yes.

I stood peering through the little glass window of the door from the waiting room. Quickly it was over and he left, and I rushed back in. She was agitated and in great distress at having been so disturbed and speaking of the doctor she said, "Oh, I hate him." It was then that she said to me, as she clutched my arm and shook it: "Don't let them wake me up again!" As far as I can remember and to the best of my knowledge, those were the last words I ever heard her utter.

She looked just like Momma when she said that, looking at me so intently with the dark eyes.

I looked at the bandage on her stomach and it seemed quite minor. She went back to sleep.

Earlier that day I had been more concerned than usual about her total lack of response. She never opened her eyes and I asked the nurse what she thought. I said it seemed to me as if she was in a coma, and the nurse agreed that she did seem to be "in a comatose state."

In that state I heard her talk out of her head and it was the only time I ever heard her do that. It was before the biopsy. She seemed perturbed about something and I heard her murmur, "I don't know how I'm going to be able to do all those dishes."

To you, Mary Ann, that seemed to be one of the saddest things of all. On her death bed, worrying about one of the little household duties she had performed over the years but would never do again.

At her house, afterwards, you called me into the kitchen with tears in your eyes and pointed to a little stack of dishes—a couple of plates and glasses and a cup or two—and said, "That's the dishes she was so worried about." So insignificant.

Dr. M. again walked into the room and silently motioned us to follow him; I knew what he was going to tell us.

Standing in the hall outside her room, James, Mary Ann and I received the news that changed our lives: "To all indications it is a cancerous tumor of the liver. The liver is enlarged about five times more than normal." I remember him saying he was reasonably sure........then, that there was nothing that could be done, only to keep her as comfortable as possible. The end could come within a week or ten days or it could be momentarily.........

Mary Ann, you and I took it with such a great calmness, didn't we? We know exactly what death is and how to deal with it. We know there is only an interlude between the time she falls asleep in death until the moment of her promised resurrection. We know there is to be loneliness and sorrow for us, the bereaved, but for her, it is only a blessed sleep till she is called back to life again by Jehovah God. We know also that we are not to judge who will receive life and who will not, but I like to remember a scripture she had marked with red pencil in her little worn Bible. It is in Malachi and it says: "At that time those in fear of Jehovah spoke with one another, each one with his companion, and Jehovah kept paying attention and listening.

And a book of remembrance began to be written up before him for those in fear of Jehovah and for those thinking upon His name."

He says He will show mercy on those who were His good and faithful servants and who showed love for Him. This she certainly did, with all her heart, and because of that we can expect her to be remembered and blessed with life in the earthly paradise.

Therefore our sorrow was softened with understanding, but not so with James. How terribly sorry I felt for him and what a blow it was for him. He had convinced himself she was going to be well, and now to receive this news........he said she was the only thing he ever loved.

Then we went out to tell the others. Good faithful Sharon was there—waiting. Andy was with her. With something akin to anger, I walked over to them and bluntly announced: "It's only a matter of hours." Later I told Sharon that I realized I shouldn't have been so abrupt and I don't know why I did that. She knew the news was bad though even before I told her. She saw us talking to the doctor. Her eyes reflected the sadness in my own and I knew she shared my sorrow with all her heart, as only a good friend can. She loved Hash.

I called you Lowell, and told you the results. You answered that you had checked and found out the very best cancer doctor around and you were going to call him right then, but finally you understood when I said, "There's no use. There is nothing that can be done now."

Then we called for Kay to get word to you, Billy. You were working in the fields, I think, and what sad news to be sent out to you.

When I called the farm to tell Gadie, Larry answered. I couldn't finish, so Alice, you took the phone and told him to tell Gadie. Later Gadie said that when he saw Larry coming toward Tracy and him out in the field where they were plowing, they knew. He and Tracy just got off the tractor and waited to hear how bad it was.

This was the only day Uncle Pal hadn't been to the hospital early—he had gone to an auction with David. I called Auntie and I can still remember the unbelieving shock in her voice when I told her it would be only a week at the most. She said she thought surely I was going to say about a year.

Bubble was there, as she had been through it all. We worried about her so much and tried to shield her somewhat, even though we always told her the truth. She is made of strong stuff though, and I've never seen her waver, even then. Her strength stabilized us, I'm sure, and we were all holding up for each other.

It was about one o'clock when we had received the biopsy news from Dr. M. and the "momentarily" came at 6:20. During that time we never left her side; we were just where we had wanted to be when the end came.

That was appropriate. She, who had given life to all five of us, had us with her when her sweet life ended. I still can't believe it........

> Very young I must have been, lying in a baby bed as
> you bent to kiss me goodbye. Wearing a black dress,
> smelling so pretty, you were going to a party—a great

rarity indeed. Loving you, feeling so close to you, I watched you leave.

Going off to school, because it was expected, even though much too soon, must have been very hard for you to accept. But you had to let me go and with eyes full of tears, you watched me leave.

Your marriage was at an end; it could not be disputed. Torn with doubts and surely confusion, you chose to go. Uncertain as to the future, as were you, I watched you leave.

Wearing a white dress, feeling so grown up, I told you good-bye as I left to be married. I don't know why you chose not to go; I hope I kissed you good-bye. Fighting not to be sentimental, knowing I'd be happy, you watched me leave.

Now you, lying in a hospital bed, were going away again. I wanted you to stay, if only you could, but I knew you had to go. I kissed you, I touched you, and softly I watched you leave.

At the onset of the final five hours of her life she was in pain, but still in an unconscious state. I wasn't in the room right then, but Lowell, you told me that she clutched at her stomach and called out in pain. You and Alice made the nurse bring a strong pain killer that the doctor had already prescribed. It immediately brought blessed relief and we never saw her show any more distress.

We were told that she would need another shot every four or five hours to kill the pain, but she never had need for even one more.

Do you feel shocked when I say that I hoped it would be quick and I was thankful that it was so brief? That's the way I had hoped the end would be. If such a thing had to occur, which it did, I couldn't have asked for it to have happened any differently.

I'm so glad she never heard the diagnosis. After he said it might be momentarily, I just knew it would be. I knew I wasn't going to leave her side either. Nothing gives me more comfort now than to remember that we were all right there beside her, touching her, speaking comforting words to her even though we didn't know if she could hear our words. Do you think she could?

They told us that hearing is the last of the senses to go, and if so, she could hear us speaking soothing words of love and appreciation to her.

Lowell, to me it was so touching to see you lean over and whisper to all of us to be careful of what we said in case she could hear. You didn't want anything at all to trouble her..........not ever again.

I often wonder why we didn't ask her to squeeze our hand if she could hear. I never though of it—I don't know if any of you did either. Thinking back on it, I believe we were all reluctant to do anything to call her back out of the long peaceful sleep she had fallen into. We didn't want to subject her to any more of the pain that came with wakefulness.

Knowing that it might be hours, Uncle Pal suggested that several of us go home with him for a short rest and some food.

Mary Ann, thinking of Tiffany, went to give her a short nap and Scarlett and Shane and Bubble went too.

Promising to call at the onset of any change, I sat by the bed, gauging her breathing. At first she had been breathing from her diaphragm but gradually it became much more shallow. Without hesitating, I called Uncle Pal to bring Mary Ann back, even though she had barely gotten there. I'm glad I did, because the end came 45 minutes later.

Bubble didn't come back; she had bid her final goodbye before she left. I had rushed down to the lobby to tell her that she should hurry up if she wanted to see her and she and Uncle Pal came in the room for the last time. That was earlier, but then her breathing leveled off and the end hadn't been as close as I thought.

They both thought it would be better if we didn't stay in the room at the end, but we all wanted to be right there.

Dr. F. came in and stood silently by the bed, having just heard the biopsy news himself. A nurse quietly took away the tubes and the needles from her body, having no further use for them.

We sat on each side of her, holding her hand, touching her hair, willing her to breath just a little longer........

Nurses slipped in and out and finally came the moment when one quietly announced that she could find no vital signs.

Still she softly breathed...........she had been a wonderful sweet mother.........how we loved her.........now everything would be perfect for her forever........

Daddy came in: "Let me hold her hand for just a minute."

He walked out and James took his place. Each breath became softer and further apart until finally........there was no more. She had slipped away from us.......softly........so softly.

## OBITUARY

Mrs. Hazel Robertson Jones, 63, wife of James Jones, Route 4, Georgetown, died Saturday evening at the Good Samaritan Hospital after a short illness.

A native of Scott County, she was the daughter of the late J. W. and Fannie Williamson Robertson and was one of Jehovah's Witnesses

Other survivors include three daughters, Mrs. Fannie Hilander, and Mrs. Alice Graves, both of Georgetown, and Mrs. Mary Ann Collins, Grayson; two sons, Billy Fields, Georgetown, and Lowell Fields, Lexington; one sister, Mrs. Mary Alice Parker, one brother, Henry D. Robertson, Lexington; eleven grandchildren and one great-grandson.

Funeral services at 10:30 a.m. Tuesday at Johnson's Funeral Home, Georgetown, by Mr. Jimmy Lizer and Mr. Nelson Collins with burial in Georgetown Cemetary.

Bearers will be David Robertson, Vaughn Reeves, Charles Reeves, Sr., Charles Reeves, Jr., Paul Hart, and Andy Anderson.

Friends may call from 4-9 p.m. today.

# 11
# TO SAY GOOD-BYE

To say good-bye to someone whom you love so very much is always hard. To say "Until next week"—"Until next year" or "Until we meet again" is difficult. But to say the final good-bye to one whom you love as yourself is surely the ultimate hurt......

A final long look at the face you love, knowing that every line and feature must be etched forever in your mind, and a last touch of the familiar hand—then you must turn and walk so far away........

Saying good-bye is indeed "hard." The death of anyone we love is hard to accept, but when that person was so full of life they fairly sparkled and they made you happy to be around them, it is doubly hard.

That's the way she was—so many people loved her. So many of them identified with her and confided in her—she seemed to fill a funny role of substitute mother and "soul sister" to a lot of people.

She was silly and funny and had a rapport with people, to a certain extent. She genuinely loved all her friends, of which I can't even begin to list. But all of you know who you are—that's what's important.

How did we ever live through such a terrible time as the visitation and the funeral the next day?

Looking back, we went through it just like it was a normal procedure and I am in awe of the memory.

Once, when I was little—very little—I followed Uncle Tom and Shirley to his barnyard to feed the cows. I was scared and I held on timidly to Shirley. (Timid is the most perfect word ever to describe me when I was small—timid—timid—timid.) I remember how they laughed when I said: "That cow will 'blow her horns' through me." When we went back to the house they repeated it to Hash and the other grown-ups, who immediately went into gales of laughter. Unable to comprehend their laughter, I looked from one to the other and pretended to join in the fun, but actually I was far removed from the situation. I just couldn't grasp what was happening; everyone knew but me.

Likewise, at the funeral home, I talked and acted aware—pretended to understand what was going on—but it was a maze of confusion to me as I looked from one face to another. Again I was the little girl in the middle of a situation that I could in no way comprehend........

There must be a form of shock that carries people through such a traumatic time—it can't be natural. I always said that if such a thing ever happened, I wouldn't be there. I'd be off somewhere in a private place, but I could not attend. So I said. Yet, there we all were, talking and visiting with friends and relatives like nothing too extraordinary had occurred.

Mary Ann, you and I discussed how we even laughed at things Charles was telling us about something we did when we were little. We were amazed later that we had "laughed." Of course he was trying to relieve some of the burden of sadness and that was fine, but in retrospect we were amazed at our laughter.

No one could have been more devastated; no one could have acted more normal. Isn't that hard to comprehend? How could we have been so calmly composed at her funeral when we were suffering such a loss?

I'm sure it has to do with the mechanism of our fantastically designed bodies; it has the unique ability to adapt to circumstances. When we experience pain, our body releases a flood of endorphins to compensate; when something too shattering to live with happens, our brain has the power to completely reject it. I'm sure you've heard of such cases.

So I suppose, in the case of death, our whole being recoils somewhat into a "private place" deep within us; therefore we are able to cope. I have seen that happen so many times to other people and I wondered how they were so calm.

There we were, in a daze, in the midst of numerous people that night at Johnson's Funeral Home.

I didn't hear this personally, but Bubble said she heard Chuck Johnson say that this was the largest funeral he had ever handled. He said the largest one his father, before him, had handled was Poppa's.

There were so many flowers—everywhere. Later I wrote cards to numerous people. It seemed so trivial to write: "Thank you for the flowers." I wanted to write: "Thank you for the love and the friendship and the caring—thank you for loving her......."

Her's was not a conventional steel casket and spray of roses which is perfectly fine and an admirable choice for most people. But she wasn't "most people."

To me, it seems that the choice of the "earthy" oak casket with it's warm golden grain and a sweet bouquet of "wild" spring flowers on it was what set the tranquil, peaceful mood more than anything else. I asked for a bunch of spring flowers that looked like they had just been picked out of a meadow and indeed they did look like that.

Never have I seen anyone who looked so beautiful and natural as she— never. Whether it is done or not, I don't know, but we sent her own make-up and rouge and her favorite lipstick to be used. They applied it beautifully; later Alice did the heartbreaking job of applying her eyebrows.

James decided on her little gold-framed glasses rather than the larger, more fashionable ones she wore more often. We all thought that was the perfect choice.

We chose one of her suits that she wore so often. It was the soft blue-grey one with a blue flowered blouse. It was just her—so natural.

Also, she had on the blue moonstone ring she liked and her wedding ring—and a new pair of pierced earrings James had given her not so long ago.

Her friends came quietly in, standing aside for a few minutes, trying to understand what had happened and trying to separate the past from the present. They couldn't comprehend that their special friend who was the most unlikely candidate imaginable for death was indeed lying there in that state.

Now, in flash backs, I see those stricken faces when I am talking to them in day-to-day life—and I remember.

Then we were sitting on the front row and Jimmy was conducting the funeral. How could such a ridiculous scene be going on? This couldn't be real. Were we acting out a charade?

Yet, there we sat—calm and quiet—all five of us in a row.

Not knowing for sure what was going through your mind, I can speak only for myself, but there I sat playing the "perfect" lady who was "perfectly composed."

I didn't want to be that way. I wanted to scream and yell and throw things. But I couldn't. If I did, how would poor Jimmy carry on? He had said in all honesty that he didn't know if he could possibly conduct it, but that he would try. You see, he loved her too.

So he stood before us, not daring to look at her beforehand, and spoke of the blessing of life and the curse of death and the meaning of it all. He explained it from the scriptures and his voice grew stronger and his face regained its color as he talked and perhaps gathered some strength from our "composure."

So I, for my part, just couldn't let him down. I sat and listened to the familiar scriptures and as you said later, Mary Ann, Hash would have been looking everyone of them up in her own Bible.

Perhaps though it would have been better had we emptied ourselves then of our pent-up sadness. Had any one of us "broken," I know we all would have. But we contained ourself.

Now I regress to that day often and have to live it over and over, because I didn't fully do it then. When I hear the songs that were played then, I simply cannot cope with them. I dissolve inside like a moth over a candle. I cannot handle the emptiness that comes upon me.

The words of one of them are:
"A thousand years, so long and passing,
To you seem but as yesterday,
But man is like the grass that blossoms,
In morning dew, then fades away.
Our years are seventy or eighty, if we have special mightiness,
Yet their insistence is on trouble, and filled they are with
    hurtfulness."

At other times when I am anywhere where there are rows of chairs, and I am sitting perfectly quiet, I have the greatest urge to grab the chair in front of me and shake it and shake it........

Not until today did I realize why—it is the latent desire to do what I wanted to do at the funeral.

Another frequent desire I have to to "fling" a cup of coffee against the wall. I haven't figured the connection to that one out yet.

Then we were at the cemetery and it is all a complete blur to me. I couldn't tell you if there were ten or one hundred people behind us; I guess I never looked around.

Nelson said a few words there and then we all left. It was all over. She was gone.

But the part that sums it all up, indeed summed up her life, I suppose, is the beautiful picture I have etched in my mind forever. I treasure it.

It is the "smile" she had on her face and the last song that was played.

Never in my life did I see a smile on a person's face after they died. Did you? But as I stood and gazed at the slight smile, which had no trace whatsoever of strain, I noticed the way her eyes turned up on the ends and crinkled ever so slightly as they always did when she smiled.

To my great delight, I realized that it was not due to any cosmetic expertise involved—it was too minute a characteristic to be duplicated! She put it there and she was at ease and at peace.

A gentle breeze moved the curtain behind her casket as the organ played these words from, "An Evening Song to Jehovah:"
"So, as this fine day ends its run,
With all our joyful service done,
Oh, may be through God's holy one
Present our evening prayer:
Jehovah God, so loving true
Accept our thanks for all you do,
Hear our intreaties, praises too,
For all your loving care."

It was then I remembered Jimmy's words to me earlier: "That little smile said it all."

*Springtime personified at eight years.*

*At 18—breaking the young men's hearts.*

*In her 20's—posing with her family (left to right): Hash, Henry, Mama, Merdie, Papa and Mary Alice.*

*Early married life.*

*Always the clown (left to right) top—*
*Mary Ann, Hash, Aunt Bea; bottom—*
*Lowell, Uncle Tom with Shirley,*
*Barbara and Fannee.*

At the "Cox Place" with Fannee, Mary and Lowell.

With Vonnie and Mary Ann—pregnant and with a far away look.

A day at the zoo—Daddy, Billy, Hash, Fannee, Mary Ann and Lowell.

*Her beloved brother Russell.*

*Late married life with Little Alice.*

*In 1973—15 year anniversary with James.*

*Feeling prissy.*

*Bubble and Uncle Pal.*

*Fannee and Gaylord—one spring.*

*Scarlett & Tracy*

*At the hospital for daily radium treatments.*

*August 1977—Vibrant health—Alice, Mary Ann, Hash and Fannee.*

*Alice, Lowell, Hash, Billy, Mary Ann, Fannee and Daddy at the Family Reunion.*

*Sparkling at the Lake Party in December.*

*With Scarlett.......and with 6 weeks to live......*

# 12
# MY THEORY

Who is to say what brings on sickness and the resultant death? I know that sin, inherited from Adam, brings death to the entire human family, but I am referring to an individual's sickness.

All her life she was confident in her vitality and it was a part of her. She was an able-bodied woman, bearing five children and increasing in vigor as the years went by—seemingly. Why did she fall victim to cancer—how could such a thing be?

Cancer is such a hard word to say. Do you, like me, avoid it as much as possible? Most people do, calling it "the big C," a terminal illness or a malignancy.

We dread it, we fear it and we speak of it in whispers. It is one of the last frontiers not yet conquered by the soldiers in white. Before my contact with it, through her, it was a mystery to me too and one I had no desire to solve.

But after such an experience, I delved into the understanding of it with a vengeance, and came up with not only an understanding of it but also less of a dread.

The book I gained this help from was given to me by my special "mentor"—Virginia Warth. For the last twenty years she has been a special friend of mine, but more so in the last five years or so. She has inspired me in all of my artistic endeavors and opened my mind's eye to many new possibilities and ideas. Most of all, she has taught me to use my imagination plus all of my senses, taught me to have an awareness of myself and my surroundings, and most importantly of all, to follow her example of daring to be somewhat different if I so desire.

Never pushing her views upon me, she has nevertheless enriched my understanding of many things simply by taking the time to share her findings with me, whether by conversation, by tape or by letter.

As to her own admission that she is always looking for "something new under the sun," being open and anxious to scan new horizons, there is no doubt that she, being around eighty years old, is one of the youngest people I know.

As I said, my understanding of cancer came from a book she gave me called "World Without Cancer—the Story of Vitamin B-17" by G. Edward Griffin.

In it I learned about the connections between cancer and the lack of nitrilosides in our modern day "lazy" diets; I learned the great importance of fresh raw vegetables and fruits.

Natural versus unnatural—that is the secret. My greatest pleasure comes from seeing Scarlett and Tracy (and Gadie) eating raw vegetables and fruit with relish, as opposed to the synthetic goodies we are deluged with (and which they still love).

When the vegetables have been grown in our own garden and are free of poisonous sprays, I find double satisfaction.

Last night Scarlett wanted a bedtime snack, and to my boundless delight, she asked for—prepare yourself—raw cauliflower and green grapes! This choice won out over her other considerations of carrots and celery. I could visualize her stomach smiling benevolently at her request.

I remember the time I was preparing apples to bake for a large group of people at the farm and after painstakingly saving all the tiny seeds in a cup to be eaten through the week, they were accidentally thrown away by some volunteer dishwasher! (No, it wasn't Puddles.)

I read that the seeds from an apple or two a day are probably sufficient to supply our bodies with the needed B-17.

Now each time I eat a seed, steam a vegetable, eliminate a fried dish or place the varied magical vitamins and herbs around the table, I am thankful that I know these things, but also wish I knew so much more.

I'd like to mention the fact that X-Rays are said to be very dangerous at times and sometimes they weaken the patient considerably at a time when they can least afford it. Stress also plays a deadly part in the development of cancer.

A simple test is available from certain doctors and is said to be 98% effective in detecting weaknesses of the body which of course can lead to the development of cancer.

In fact, I recently underwent one such test and sincerely believe it is worth recommending. Anything that fights cancer is worth recommending, wouldn't you say?

I knew nothing about cancer when Hash first discovered she had it in early 1975. She had gone with James to Dr. Wells; he for back trouble—she for a pap smear. It was the first one she ever had and she considered it unnecessary; the reason she went was almost too inconsequential to be considered.

One morning she called me, with an uneasy tone to her voice, which I later recognized as fear, telling me she had to go to Dr. Wells office to discuss the result of the pap smear which had come back showing some kind of trouble. This was in early '75, probably January or February.

In my optimistic ignorance, I never expected anything to come from that; it was just a mistake—something to be straightened out right away. Nothing was wrong—I was positive of that. After all, hadn't everything always "turned out alright"?........

Can you understand that I sincerely did believe that? I did, because all my life, everything literally did turn out alright. Not only alright—but perfect.

During childhood I was surrounded by all the love and warm security I needed; in the adolescent years I was still content and happy even though I was painfully introverted away from my family.

Being such a "good" little girl, I was in turn treated "good" by most everyone. Daddy even called me "Queenie" as I turned into a teenager, thus symbolizing my attitude toward life. I was a "queenie" of all I surveyed—life was good. (My first year of High School was a completely different matter, but not one to be dealt with here.)

Then I met and married Gadie, thus continuing my "perfect" life. We have always been happy and very importantly, compatible.

Scarlett and Tracy were born, healthy and strong—a boy and a girl—just what I ordered.

No pitfalls—no problems. All was well.

Do you remember hearing about the old lamplighters that would go through the towns, long ago, and light the street lamps at dusk? Then, on the hour, as they walked through the quiet streets, they would sing out "Nine o'clock and all is well!" And so on through out the night.

Well, that is what my life reminded me of; my life was the quiet town and all was well. Did I really expect it to last all through the night, all through my life? I suppose I did—I've always been terribly naive.

When I was very small, I used to pray that our two grandmothers——Momma and Mommau—would never die. Just simply that—never die—even though they were both rather old at the time. Even then, I sensed the change that death would make to my young life and I feared the change, as of course we all do.

Now, back to the consultation with Dr. Wells; he said there definitely was trouble and he wanted her to go right on to Lexington to see a doctor whom he highly recommended, Dr. G.

Later, after she died, we were looking through her pictures and little things she kept. She kept very little; therefore what we saw had more significance. There was a little piece of paper that had been scribbled on; it was on the back of a bill or a receipt and on it she had written: Heard test result—Dr. Wells—scared.

She was "scared." I never ever wanted her to be scared. How well she concealed it—confiding in no one—holding it all in. What stress that must have caused.

At the appropriate time, James and I went with her to Dr. G's office and she was tested and found out that, indeed, it was a malignant tumor of the cervix. It was cancer.

I couldn't believe it! I kept waiting for them to admit it had to be some mistake and that they were wrong! This was, honestly, the very first time for me that things had not worked out alright! Believe me.

Next, I had to find an escape, a safety valve, something to cling to in this time of wrongness. I found it in the doctor's plan for treatment: There would be radiation treatments every day for, as well as I remember, a month. I believe it was about twenty-five treatments in all. Then there would be a radium transplant for her which included a hospital stay of a few days. Then the malignancy would be obliterated and she would be back to normal!

Even though I consider myself a fairly intelligent person, I can look back and see times when I reacted quite to the contrary.

Now I know that a diagnosis like that could be right as well as it could be wrong. So much depends upon the circumstances, the person, the time element and the reactions involved. Indeed, it depends on the diet and the outlook itself of the person involved.

But then, I knew nothing of this. I only knew she would take the treatments prescribed and come back to us as she had always been, and this whole thing would then be over and behind us, where it belonged.

Before I go any further, I must say that, with cancer there are many, many people who do become cured. That is a fact and cures are quite common—final, definite cures. You probably all know of many such cases.

So I am not in any way here saying that she was doomed from the start because she had cancer; I am saying that I should have allowed for that possibility, but I did not. In my schedule for her recovery, there was no room for doubt.

Again, I want to stress this point: I didn't even consider the fact that she might have a recurrence and as far as I was concerned, the last treatment would be the end of the whole thing.

Full of this confidence, I took my turns at taking her to the Medical Center for the radium treatments. If I knew then what I know now, I would have headed in the exact opposite direction with her—anywhere away from that despicable radiation.

The tumor was a foreign thing and none of us could identify with it. Through all of this, she had no pain whatsoever connected with the tumor; to us it was unreal and she even said she felt the whole thing was completely unnecessary. (In this, perhaps she was displaying an inborn wisdom. Statistics show that patients who receive no treatment at all live just as long—or longer—than those who subject themselves to radiology or chemotherapy. Orthodox cancer therapies treat the symptoms (the tumor) rather than the cancer.)

The time for her to go into the hospital for the radium transplant coincided with a preplanned trip to Mexico for Gadie and me. Linda and

Freddie Gillispie had asked us to go along with them months before we even knew of her dilemma.

Naturally, she adamantly insisted that we go on. Mary Ann, you left your own family to come here to stay with Scarlett and Tracy, and Alice, you came too. Between the two of you, you handled the children involved and went back and forth to the hospital to visit her.

After the simplicity of the daily radium treatments she was unprepared for the terrible ordeal of the transplant.

Being an uncomplaining woman, the two statements she made spoke volumes. One, which I heard indirectly, was that she said she "went through a living hell." The other: "Oh, I wish Fannee hadn't gone to Mexico." That statement went through me like a knife when I heard it.

How I resent her being treated like a guina pig with that horrible transplant. Yes, I mean just that—she was used in an experimental program as I found out later.

Several months after she died, I read an article in the Lexington Herald. It told about the new radium transplant that they were "experimenting" with on a certain number of patients. They were pleased to announce that it had been 50% effective. Fifty percent!

So the ordeal was over and behind her and life proceeded as normal. We were blessed with having her for three more years.

If only I had known then what I know now, I would have approached the situation so much differently.

Our bodies are constantly bombarded by carcinogenic substances; what chance do our poor "imposed upon" bodies have? More than you would think, if we just give them half a chance and supplement them with the necessary things that have been taken away from us daily. Doesn't it make sense that if we want to fight an internal enemy, we should use natural things such as minerals and herbs that are composed of the same matter as we are? Why impose upon our bodies the death-dealing chemicals and radium; why not fight with natural substances that we can easily absorb and be fortified with?

I know of a fabulous herbal program that is fully effective and if I should develop cancer I would be able to face it with no great dread—I would simply go into the treatment of it with this marvelous herbal program and of equal importance—a positive mental attitude!

More and more has been acknowledged recently in the vital role our amazing mind plays on the recovering and the maintaining of health. I firmly believe that.

If you believe, "I am well and healthy" and if your mind can convince your body of that, all is well. Why not try it—eliminate stressful situations and think good thoughts—enjoy life.

I have just learned about another mavelous program called SPC—Self Programmed Control, taught by Dr. Alfred A. Barrios. It's worth looking into.

I have learned so much and want to learn so much more—anything to get us through the last spasms of this dying old world.

There are so many self-help avenues available: Reflexology, biofeedback, herbal programs, proper use of vitamins and minerals, acupressure, kinesiology, chelation therapy, iridology, etc. If you just make yourself aware of your surroundings and what is going on, you can learn so much. Reach out and learn—don't stagnate in one old routine.

I am taking a marvelous course now on "How to deal with stress", conducted by Dr. Walt Stoll and from it I am learning wonderful things. However, just reading books on various subjects and listening to people who have experimented with things can be just as educational.

If I had known these things back then, I would also have helped Hash with a special diet which would have been rich in nitriloside content and which would have included such things as millet, buckwheat, sorghum, elderberry jelly, stewed prunes, apricot brandy, barley, lentils,and so on.

This would have been supplemented with high dosages of vitamin C and E, plus natural multi-vitamins.

Along with this, if necesssary, I would have taken her anywhere in the country, or out of it, to be treated with Laetrile. I would do exactly the same for myself, if necessary, and I have great confidence that it would be the very wisest choice open to any person suffering from cancer today.

The ensuing three years were routine and normal and free from worry as far as I was concerned; I felt certain they were for her too, up until the last few months.

Some splendid examples of her "supposedly" remarkable health are the beautiful pictures taken at our family reunion in late August of 1977, just a little over seven months before she died.

They were taken by a photographer friend, Alan Breeze, and they show her as a beautiful vibrant woman, full of good health and glowing color.

In fact, we all agreed that in the small family pictures, she looked far better and much more attractive than any of us, her three daughters.

How thankful I am that we had that reunion, and more importantly, that we listened to Daddy when he insisted that we have the "original" family pictures taken. His prophetic words were: "I want a picture taken of you kids with your mother and me, because it might be the last chance we'll ever have to do it."

Later, most of us agreed that if the above statement came true, we would have thought about Daddy dying perhaps, but not Hash........I told Daddy that if ever he did anything really right in his life, his insistence on those pictures must have been it.

Still speaking of stress, I would like to mention this incident that showed me how real stress is. However, I didn't understand what was happening to me until months after it was over. I kept dreading the first anniversary of her death, April 8. As the date came closer and closer, I built up such an anxiety I could hardly stand it. I did not want it to be a year past, two and then three. I resented that and I tried to hold it back. But the day came and I got through it, but then that night, I began to expel water through my eyes and my nose and it was like a never-ending fountain—it was constant! I couldn't understand it, I had no cold and I never had allergies. After two whole weeks it finally subsided and I was back to normal. Then later I heard that our body can build up stress to such an extent that it finally has to be expelled in some way; in some cases it comes out like mine did, rather than in sickness and disease and for that I am thankful.

I feel that some of the points that I learned from Dr. Stoll are important enough to be listed here; don't we need all the help we can get?

Stress, being one of our greatest enemies today, plays havoc with our physical and mental well-being.

Here is a list of ten ways to combat stress:
1. Recognize that death is an imminent possibility.
2. Accept responsibility for our own happiness.
3. Look for truth and don't just seek reaffirmant of our own ideas.
4. Face your weaknesses and grow.
5. Spend some time alone—get in touch with your "inner core"—your unchangeable essence.
6. Read about spiritual things and think spiritual thoughts.
7. Strengthen your religious ties.
8. Ask the deep unasked questions—think deeply.
9. Seek balance and harmony in your life.
10. Realize that "the journey" is the important thing.

Surprisingly, Hash had gone along with most of the above suggestions. She realized that God promises, as recorded in the Bible, that soon all the woes and sorrows and injustices will be completely done away with and the earth will be a paradisaic place to live with perfect eternal life in view. She embraced that hope and in so doing she found the answers to the "deep unasked questions" and she assumed responsibility for her own happiness. Perhaps she was way ahead of all of us.

Dr. Stoll said that we *are* our brother's keeper and with that I agree. We must be aware of one another and be concerned; it's wrong to be so tied up in ourself that we are unaware of our fellowman's suffering. Often we have eyes that do not see and ears that do not hear........

He said we should visualize reality and in so doing, we can create reality. According to him, avoiding reality and living in an unreal world causes stress. As of now, I can't agree with him on that point; my dream world was fine as long as it lasted........

So whether to praise or to damn the treatment involved is really beside the point now; it is much too late for her, but not for us. We have a chance to choose, and we must choose wisely.

Four words, uttered by Dr. M., almost drove me to distraction from the time I heard them till the time I accepted them, almost three months later. The words were: "I am 'reasonably' sure" and were said after the biopsy, when he was telling us that she had a tumor of the liver.

I didn't like the uncertainty of the word "reasonably" and I didn't like the questions that arose in my mind. I didn't like the doubt and the fears that accompanied it and I was consumed with the desire to change it to another word—a definite word.

The way I finally did accomplish that desire was to follow through on the despised autopsy report—a long dragged out process that took about three months of agony.

I have mixed emotions about the autopsy itself. A request for permission to do it was presented to James at his very weakest moment and he at first refused it. Then they gave their reason for wanting it—the possibility that it was a hereditary thing that might effect us—and that prompted him to give his permission, albeit against his will.

It was all settled before I even knew of the request; it wasn't my place to grant or deny permission anyhow, but I would have fought it. Then I would have had to wonder for the rest of my life and to be tormented by questions. As it turned out, I realized one day, soon after the first week or so, that in the autopsy report would lie the answers to all my burning questions.

I could not wait to find out what were the true reasons for her relatively sudden death—but wait I did. Wait and wait and wait.

As is the case with all of us, the more I waited the more suspenseful I became; I was obsessed with what "might" have happened. Mistakes, wrong diagnosis, hasty conclusions, faulty X-Rays—they all crossed my mind. They all loomed large, as possibilities.

I'm sure I was a complete nuisance to Dr. M.'s secretary. I called several times weekly to find out if the results were in and I called the Pathology department at the hospital weekly.

They kept "putting me off" for different reasons (reasons to them, but excuses to me).

I just knew they had discovered that something went wrong and didn't want to reveal it. Just as I was ready to call a lawyer to demand to see the long overdue results, word came that they were in. Arrangements were made for Alice and me to meet with Dr. M. to discuss the report.

I was almost sick as we drove to Lexington, being so nervous and tense, and the waiting in his office seemed an eternity.

All my uncertainties and anxieties were for naught however when I had the official report. Here are portions of it:

"This patient died from carcinoma of the pancreas with massive metastasis to the liver and extensive metastasis to the lung.....scattered throughout the lungs were numerous tumor nodules.....the liver was three to four times the normal size and almost completely replaced by tumor....there are some large bizarre tumor giant cells.....multiple sections of the pancreas show very extensive pancreatitis of an acute nature.....

So it was official. Her body had been completely ravaged with the dreaded cancer. It's still hard to believe....

Her decline was so terribly fast, or should I say mercifully fast? I'm quite certain of the reason. I read the following words about the effect that radiation has on a person's health in the "World Without Cancer" book:.........."There is often an explosive or fulminating increase in the biological malignancy of his lesion. This is marked by the appearance of diffuse metastases and a rapid deterioration in general vitality followed shortly by death."

The above seems to have applied to her, especially the part about a rapid deterioration in general vitality.

My theory is that the radiation weakened her vital organs to such an extent that, even though her body put up a tremendous fight and seemingly won the battle over the three year period, in the end its terribly weakened state prevailed and death came soon after.

The above is my theory; perhaps you have another. Actually, all the words in our vocabulary are to no avail on the subject of death—they are just that—words.

The Bible puts our life and our death in the proper perspective when it says: ".......whereas you do not know what your life will be tomorrow. For you are a mist appearing for a little while and then disappearing."

In conclusion then, I suppose that rather than cursing the "time and circumstances" that took her away, we should instead be very happy that we were blessed with having her as long as we did, for blessed we surely were.

# 13
# HER LEGACY TO US

When a person dies, often their worth is gauged by what they left behind. In the materialistic world we find ourself in, material worth is more often valued over other things.

In this aspect, she fell quite short. In fact, many times I have heard her jokingly remark: "When I die, all I will have to leave for you kids is my A-hole and my elbow."

However, we know she left more, much more, than that. She left us with memories, ideals, laughter, and mainly—hope.

Which one of us could ever feel intimidated by death now, after having seen her face it so well and knowing her expectation of what is to come?

For me, it put death in its proper perspective:

I never really knew death before.
I had only a nodding acquaintance with it;
It was to be considered neither friend nor foe.
It was far from my flighty mind
and having no time for such thoughts,
I flipped through life with ease.

Then one day I saw death face-to-face
and never will I be the same.
Still, I cannot classify it as friend or foe.
It does have a sting
and it is an enemy in most ways.
It stole a most precious possession
that cannot be retrieved.

> But it was a friend
> in that it gave some subtle warning before it struck
> and most importantly of all
> it left in such a gentle way.

Hash had no particular ideas on death; she was much more concerned with life. However, she understood death and evidently had no undue dread of it; it was just a part of Jehovah's grand pattern—life, death, life again. She believed this—she taught this to others—she taught this to us.

One of the persons she helped to understand this wonderful philosophy, albeit a Biblical philosophy, was a friend named Francis.

I talked with Francis several months after Hash died, and this is what she told me: She discovered she had cancer and she became almost too frightened to live; she could think of nothing else and was unable to even sleep at night. Then she met Hash and after hearing her wonderful philosophy, never again was she the same. Hash told her that "the doctors don't know it all" and maybe it wasn't as bad as they said. Then she taught her from the Bible that even if it should be a sickness "unto death," that wouldn't be the end, and she could have a glorious future ahead of her with perfect health—forever. So wholeheartedly did Francis embrace this new hope, that she overcame her dreadful overwhelming fear and in her words: "I just got to where I didn't even worry much about it anymore." Indeed, the doctors didn't "know it all" since this was over fifteen years ago and Francis is fine now. So she looks back and remembers her good friend who lovingly helped her through the difficult period of her life.......she taught her not to be afraid.

Another thing that we should appreciate is this: After we all became the persons we now are, we were accepted as such: The good, the bad and the ugly!

Now, seriously, we were each individuals and she did accept us for what we were. Recognizing the fact that we are all accountable for ourself, she didn't meddle and try to bring out impossible and improbable changes.

Another highly commendable virtue that she had was appreciation! Whether it was inborn or cultivated I don't know; I can't remember when she was without it.

She often talked to me about the importance of appreciation; I, in turn, have desperately tried to impress upon Scarlett and Tracy the importance of it.

There are few things in life worse than an unappreciative child, in my opinion and I am grateful that both Scarlett and Tracy have cultivated this fine quality.

I must admit that sometimes their appreciation is in disguise and quite subtle, but it is there nevertheless. An example is the note Scarlett left for me one morning. I had left at seven-thirty with Gadie; I didn't want to miss the round-up of around 160 cattle which were being taken to market. It was a fine morning—I served coffee from a thermos and donuts and took movies of the event. Conrad Haynes was there to help and I felt just like one of the men, with my long underwear on and cowboy boots.

When I got home, I found this note on the table:

> "Mom,
> I didn't have any breakfast because I couldn't find anything decent. I'll have to eat that rotten food at school because you weren't here to fix my lunch. My clothes probably look terrible because you weren't here to tell me what looks good. My hair looks like Shirley Temple because you weren't here to roll it for me. And I'll probably miss the bus because you weren't here to watch for it. And how was your morning?
>
> Scarlett."

And then at other times, the appreciation is so outspoken it makes it all worthwhile.

Gadie and I received a card in the mail; on the front was a little duck and the words: A Message of Thanks.

Inside were these beautiful words:

> Mom and Dad,
> Thank you so much for being the perfect parents. I'll never forget all the wonderful things you have done for me. There is nothing that I want or need that I don't already have. You have taught me consideration and respect which are very important. Thank you for doing everything in your power to make me happy.
>
> Scarlett

And then on the back page were these words:

> Mom and Dad,
> Thanks so much for everything you have gotten and done for me. Beating, and flicking my head, has taught me a lot. Your the best Mom and Dad in the whole world.
>
> Love,
> Tracy

Hash appreciated all five of us and accepted us for what we were. She was grateful for any attention we gave her; she never demanded any more or indeed, never seemed to need or want any more than what we gave.

When I was little and she was about the age I am now, I heard her proud words to a childhood friend she had run into: "I have five children." They were comparing notes on their lives and the friend seemed surprised to hear that she had five children and still looked so young and attractive. The pride in her voice always stuck in my mind and made an impression on me even back then, thus, pride in her family is another virtue I remember her for.

In numerous families, indeed, in the majority of families, there exists an undercurrent of jealousy and back-biting when the various members become simultaneously adult and diverse in their opinions.

However, to my delight, we haven't done this, have we? Voicing disapproval over things is different than engaging in lies and dishonesties and stirring up agitations. Our relationship, as to the five of us, has been devoid of such shenanigans and I am so happy for that.

I can honestly say that I never heard Hash say one unkind word about any of you, not one cutting word of criticism or one insinuation to me behind your back. That is the mark of a good woman; what she said to your face is another matter!

To clarify this further—she didn't have to bridle her tongue and hold herself in check to keep from denouncing any of us—it was just not her nature to do so. Neither, I think, is that inclination in any of us.

Also, while on the subject, I am so glad to be able to say that I can't recall any of us ever saying one sharp or unkind word to her, or speaking to her with disrespect in our voices. I'm not saying it never happened, reasonably it did at times, but it would have been a rarity when it did.

I remember once when I became a teenager, probably that numb age of fourteen that I remember so well, I said something to her that must have been sharp or hateful. I would give anything if I could remember what it was, but I can't. Nevertheless, I'll never forget what her reply was: "I never thought I'd hear "little Fannee" talk to me like that."

Well, those simple words and the way she looked when she said them completely eradicated any such further words from me—ever. How glad I am that she "broke" me there at the start from such ways. I know that never again did I ever speak to her in any such way, neither by word nor look nor action.

You little grandchildren, please remember how important respect is in the family arrangement. Parents deserve respect because that is God's plan for a happy family.

If perhaps, you feel you're not showing the proper respect now, it is never too late to cultivate it and you will never regret it. In time, your parents will show you respect too.

It makes everything so much "nicer," and when you have an occasion to "look back" like I am now, think how much better you will feel.

So that is something we should all respect her for and remember her for: she unconsciously looked for the good in each of us, accepting us and loving us for what we were. What more could we have asked?

In summation then, her legacy to us was her unequivocal ideas on life and living that she found in the Bible. It was her positive outlook on life; her theory that, indeed, everything would work out alright. Perhaps it did, after all.

## SEE FOREVER

Look at her with eyes aglow,
confident and oh so sure.
Never doubting what she knew—
If only we can be the same.

Never one to hold it back—
Spoke her piece and spoke it well.
Words tumbled out, not always in order
But words of truth and full of fire.

Intelligent she was and so well-read
And blessed with an abundance of friends.
Children who showed love and above all, respect.
Demanding nothing of us but grateful for all we gave.

Eyes that were dark and witty and sly,
So ready to laugh and have fun.
Anxious to talk and go here and there,
But with feelings so easily hurt.

A vibrant woman—full of good health........
Ah.......therein we see her deceit.
But was it a deceit of her or of us—
Not even time will tell.

So now we look back—we reminisce—we cry.
But even as we do, we can also laugh,
To have been so blessed as surely we were,
Having a mother with eyes that could see forever.

# 14
## CONTINUITY

As far as I am concerned, continuity means children and grandchildren. Life goes on; a generation comes and a generation goes.....

The things that are passed down, the ideas, the resemblances, and the hopes merge silently into various ones and reappear years later, without warning and without apology. Who shall we blame; who shall we thank? Must we not accept our destiny, even as we curse our genes? Or shall we bask in our achievements as ours alone, even as we ignore our impetus?

I have a little plague that says:

"I have no fear of tomorrow, for I have seen yesterday and I love today."

I too have seen yesterday, but I desire to look at it again, from time to time. It means something to me—I never want to completely let it go. I want this continuity; it is something I fight for. You have only to witness my promoting of the two family reunions held yearly, the Fields' and the Robertson's, to understand my heartfelt desire for continuity.

There is a scripture in the Bible that always made Hash laugh. It speaks of an ablebodied man who filled his quiver with arrows and it compared the arrows to his offspring.

She had a small scale quiver of grandchildren—eleven of them and she loved them all dearly. She was their "Hashie Bug."

Lowell and Amanda had the first two grandchildren—Marie and Lindsay Clay, and then later Marjorie.

Marie was her very first one. Little Marie—a—ree as I used to call her when she was the age Shane is now, four years old. She would stay here with me for a week, once in a while, and I loved her so. She was so little and solemn-eyed and I would fix tea parties in the front yard for her and a little neighbor boy. I have a picture of them "having tea." She was born July 5, 1960 in Nicholasville. Now she is married to Bruce Goodrich and has a baby of her own, little Chris who was the only great grandchild Hash ever knew. Since Hash's death he has been joined by a baby sister, little Kikki.

Next in Lowell's family came Lindsay Clay, born February 18, 1963 in Millersburg.

To me, Lindsay is a carbon copy of you, Lowell. When he visits us, to watch him walk and talk takes me back to when we were all at home together and I see you all over again.

I think of Lindsay as a wild young Indian, hiding his true face from the world. But soon he'll be a man and we'll be proud of what he becomes. He'll develop in his own due time.

Next came Marjorie, born February 28, 1964 in the Georgetown Hospital. There are just 25 days between her and Scarlett, and that was the first time I went out of the house after Scarlett was born, to go to the hospital to see her and to visit Amanda.

To me, Margie looks more like Hash than any of the grandchildren and to my delight, Margie and Scarlett are very special bosom friends. They have a special closeness that only cousins can; Hash and Jesse had it; Shirley and I had it; Scarlett and Margie have it.

Margie has the wonderful qualities of kindness and mildness and as I have often told her—she is just plain sweet.

The next two grandchildren are Scarlett and Tracy, born to Gaylord and me.

Scarlett Lee was born in the Georgetown Hospital on February 3, 1964. She looked like a little rosebud when she was born, and has always been a great source of pleasure to me. I would say she, my first born, is everything a daughter should be. She and I take up where Hash and I left off......

Her great passion is horses and she is involved in all aspects of the "love of horses" from the desire to "show them" down to the trimming of their hooves. But, being extremely versatile, she can go directly from her "horse shoes" to her ballet shoes.

Tracy Bronston was born on August 30, 1967, in Central Baptist Hospital in Lexington. He's my little helper and is a combination of a clown and a skilled laborer. If he should be described in one word I would choose "capable." That he is and I would feel perfectly at ease in trusting this "child of my heart" with most anything, even though he's only eleven years old.

Mary Ann and Nelson have contributed Justin, Rachel, and the last grandchild, Tiffany.

Justin was born on June 30, 1968 in Pike County, Kentucky, just across the Tug River from West Virginia. I love that word, Tug River. Remember the Hatfields and the McCoys and how the Tug River played such an important part?

Justin is the sort of child who went into business of his own at the age of five or six. He sold cards and seeds and detergents and could trade you out of your eye-teeth if he so desired. He is a child with great capabilities, and he is the "little black-eyed genius" of the family.

Rachel is soft and gentle; a sensitive child who resembles Hash in looks. She was born November 8, 1970 in Hinton, West Virginia.

Rachel is the sort of child who brings great comfort to a parent and warms your heart. She also is showing an inclination to be quite poetic and artistic in keeping with her nature.

Little Tiffany Chantel—the last grandchild Hash was to know was born on December 22, 1977 in Huntington, West Virginia. She is a dark-eyed, all knowing enigma of a child, yet to be discovered. She is a bonus, bringing happiness to many. Looking deep into her dark, velvet eyes, I sometimes feel she has the answer to all our questions.

How thankful you were Mary Ann, that Hash lived to see and share "Little Tiffany"—for a little over three months.

Cheryl and Timmy were born to Billy and Betty.

Timmy, born on May 9, 1966 at Cynthiana is a strong determined "little man" and one to be proud of.

He too has been entrusted with many early responsibilities and has come through with flying colors. These qualities are enhanced by his politeness and his great consideration of others; such are the "makings of a man."

Cheryl is the "nature girl" who loves all of God's creations and has rapport with bugs and beast alike. She was born in Georgetown on July 27, 1967.

Cheryl listens to the wind and writes down its words; she communicates wih the earth. Having such qualities, she'll never be bored with life, nor bore others with hers.

Born to Alice and Butch Graves on July 31, 1974 was Shane Scott. He arrived at the Central Baptist Hospital in Lexington.

I love this little razor-sharp, perceptive, white-headed child as if he were my .own. An example of his sharp sensitivity and ability to communicate with adults is what he said in trying to comfort different ones of us after Hash's death: "Don't cry. You know we'll get to see Granny Hash at the resurrection." He was only three years old.

Not long ago I painted a picture of Peter Pan and around it, on the canvas, I glued pictures of the eleven grandchildren. They were all captured in one mystical moment of time, by the eye of the camera, and I called it "Forever Young." Peter Pan was gazing wistfully in at the world of reality, one which he would never know, but which these children know so well.

Pictures figure prominently in my life—I consider them a visible lifeline to the past. I have a valuable, albeit small, collection of portraits at the farm of our "Roots." I have large pictures of Mommau and Poppau

Fields, of Momma and Poppa Robertson, and two fabulous portraits Daddy gave me of Great-Grandmother Annie Warford and Great Grandfather John Morris. Then Kay presented me with the masterpiece of my collection—one of our great-great-grandmother, Eliza Warford, sitting in a highbacked chair.

To my surprise, we have a chair almost identical to the one in the picture so I plan to have my picture taken, sitting in that chair, wearing a long black dress similar to hers and wearing the SAME earrings she has on in the picture! Kay still has them—isn't that marvelous?

John Hockensmith, a fabulous photographer here in Georgetown, is going to take the picture of me and with a process at which he is extremely adept, he can "age" the picture to where I will look like her contemporary! (Now that I think of it, I'm not too fond of the whole idea—me a contemporary of an eighty year old woman......!)

Gadie has a fantastic big black Rolls Royce that belonged to a Lord of England; it is in perfect shape, and I'm wild about it. It is the epitome of luxury. If I had to choose between it and those ancestor pictures at the farm, guess what I'd choose! Now I have you wondering, don't I? Well, just keep wondering!

So now, even though Hash's physical presence is gone, all the other things connected with her—the things she believed in, her attitude toward life, her love for us—live on and make us remember her vividly.

So I suppose we can say that "Granny Hash" will always be, in many senses of the word, "forever young."


## CONTINUITY

Looking so radiant and pretty,
You are obviously in the prime of your life.
We have a happy time together;
Good friends always do, especially
    being mother and daughter.
Life is very good; a perfect future looms.

Perfection in the highest sense of the word.
We never ask—"how do you feel?"
That is no part of our life—
    we who are blessed with health.

My eyes, glazed with your philosophy, fail to see your
    Steps begin to falter, ever so imperceptively.
Life marches on—when did you begin to fall
    out of step?
Time changes before my eyes—in wonderment I
    see the lines appear.

Older ones go and young ones arrive and I see
    the children bloom like flowers.
Must we so soon be the older generation?
Why, as they are growing golden,
must we be growing gray............?

# 15
# LOWELL'S CHAPTER

Lowell Scott—the first born. Of course you were first—you probably shoved us all back and dared us to move—prenatally!

The world was introduced to you on February 16, 1939.

Knowing you, we can understand why you felt you had to come into the world in a big way—but ten pounds!? That was enough to get everyone off to a rough start!

Being born in a hospital was not the "only way" back then; you were born at Momma and Poppa's house where Hash and Daddy lived.

Attending the good Dr. Sanford was Momma, Aunt Betty and the ever faithful Bubble. You were named for Lowell Thomas.

One thing that always puzzled me is the fact that even though you were born a little more than a year after their marriage, you always insisted you saw them marry and in some way a merry-go-round was involved. Very interesting, I must say.

Your memory came into clearer focus involving the time you lived in Lexington at Mrs. Lakes' house. According to you, there was only one room in the house, the bathroom, where the "evil" old landlady could not eavesdrop on you through the walls.

You would play in a big box and hide in it from Daddy when he came in from work.

Boxes figured quite prominently in your young childhood; I recall the different size boxes you would tie together like a train and pull them from the Cox's place to the store—probably full of groceries on the return trip.

After we were grown, you revealed how "ashamed" you were of us all "strung" out along the road. All children go through stages of being ashamed of various things, so you are forgiven.

However, one thing that I can't forgive you for is your being ashamed of me when I was in the first grade and you were across the hall in Mrs. Blackburn's third grade.

You came home one day and related your abject embarrassment to Hash with these words: "I was out in the hall with all my friends and there stood Fannee with her pants hanging down under her dress!"

Now really, what could you expect from a timid little first grader who was incidently wearing the short, short little dresses in style then? I can't forgive you for not coming over and knotting the elastic at the top; I probably drooped around like that all day.

Seriously though, Hash always kept us spic and span and she was very diligent about the fit of our clothes. She always laid out my clothes to wear to school and I never ever deviated from her choice. In fact, I was so meek that even when I disliked some outfit, I would not have ever dreamed of saying so or to have expressed my opinion. Why I was so timid I'll never know because Hash would have been more than glad to have me wear whatever I liked; she would never have intimidated me in any way. I would actually walk to catch the bus past Kay's and cry on the way because of what I had on! Can you imagine such timidity? Years later I told Hash about that and she was absolutely stricken........

You were quite a fashion plate yourself, what with the little short pants and the sailor suit and the angora berets, etc. The "first born" always has a great variety of pictures taken, and along down the line they decrease in frequency until the later chidlren are photographed scarcely at all. That's true even in my case of only two children.

So there are smiling little pictures of you here and there, in the cedar chest and in the relative's albums, even on the post office wall!

Like most little boys, you dreamed of being a hero someday, performing some stupendous feat that would perhaps be recorded in a book for all to read.

Well, you got your chance when you were about four years old—but you blew it with a slip of your tongue.

Hash was pushing me in a baby buggy in Lexington where we lived and somehow you saw that I was in the path of an oncoming car. With superhuman speed and daring courage, you managed to maneuver my buggy out of the path of certain death, thereby eliciting for yourself the noble title of "hero." However, when you stood ready to receive your accolades, you announced to one and all, with perhaps an uncanny foreknowledge of things to come—"I'm a heathen!"

Kools cigarettes—you remember when Hash smoked them, don't you? In fact, when I enquired as to your fondest memory of long ago, you decided that it was your remembrance of her grabbing you up and hugging you when you had brought her some Kools.

Like most little boys, you too had a wooden wagon; you used it to pull groceries from the store to the Cox Place. (Perhaps the boxes were temporarily out of commission.)

Once, while playing, you crammed a little ring on your finger, and as sometimes happens, it wouldn't come off. As Hash grabbed you by the hand, you dimly heard her say, "come on, we'll go down to the store and get it cut off!" That was all you needed to completely panic—they were going to cut your finger off!!

Bolting away from her like a little wild animal, you ran and hid in the tall weeds, crying. She found you, as mothers always do, and took you to Hans Cox's little shop where he carefully cut it off, leaving the finger intact! What a relief!

A good example of the constant mischief you were in and of how that mischief often backfired on you is the time you almost set the old porch at the Cox Place on fire.

Dorothy and Omaria Houston were sitting on the porch with Hash and Daddy; they were talking about the crops and the canning, no doubt, when Omaria noticed that his pants leg had started to scorch! A quick investigation revealed that you and Kenny (and I) were having a fine time under the wooden porch with a penny box of matches, a cigar and a cigarette. But to our surprise, and ultimately to our despair, somehow the porch above us started to ignite. The fire under the porch was quickly extinguished; not so quickly though the fire on Kenny's backside, I'm afraid. I, being the sweet little innocent bystander, was not punished; as for you, the last report they had that night was that you were still running..........

"Pete" was the little black and white dog that belonged to Hash. How she loved Pete! I have a picture of her—pregnant and wearing a "smock"—with Aunt Mabel beside her and Pete at her feet. You say you remember when Pete died and how Hash cried and cried. He died of old age.

Just five days ago we lost our good sweet dog—Cimmaron, our fine three year old German Shepherd. She died in labor—such a needless loss. I could never feel empathy before for people who lost a dog or cat—I had never experienced it, therefore I couldn't understand their sadness. But now I do and I understand Hash crying over Pete......Harlan buried Cimmaron in a beautiful spot in the side yard at the farm, under a big old tree. We all miss good old Cimmaron; sometimes, dogs are people too. One of my first thoughts after she died was how Hash would hate to hear the news.......

Company was coming—it was Sunday and you and I were dressed in our best clothes. Hash was cooking dinner—I could smell the fried chicken in the house—Mommau's house. We were sitting on the cedar chest, playing with little "spool tractors" you had made by notching empty spools and tightening a rubber band around them........we were at the Cox

Place and we saw Bubble coming. Out from under the porch we crawled—
.our special playground—and never have we been so dirty! Hash and
Bubble laughed so hard as Hash seriously asked Bubble: "Are they even
worth cleaning up?"

Hash fainted easily; so do I. I can recall an image of us being at a circus
and standing inside a tent with people packed tightly around us. All of a
sudden, she had fainted; I suppose it was because of the closeness and the
lack of air.

Once she fainted, for no special reason, and you were with her. You
were very young, and when she opened her eyes and saw you standing over
her, she asked you what had happened. I remember her laughter as she told
us many times what your reply had been: "*I* hit you. I've always wanted to
do it!" What a devious little mind! How did you even come up with such an
idea at your tender age?

You told me about the two of us cleaning up the kitchen for her,
probably doing the dishes in our very childish way, and then hiding as she
walked into the kitchen and feigned great surprise at the "results." You said
she would always decide some little "Brownies" had slipped in. Does
anyone else ever call fairies "Brownies" or was that our special name for
them?

You remember a sandbox at Bubble's house, Poppa, and Cracker Jacks
and the reunion. Do you remember Billy and Jimmy Robertson? I do.

The yearly Robertson reunion—it is pressed between the pages of my
mind like a treasured picture—a faded old water color to take out time after
time and admire. It was the high point of the year for Shirley and me, she
having the same sense of family I have. Of course then we were too young to
think of it in that way—we just liked the idea of a big crowd, the good food
and the excitement of it all!

Hash and Aunt Bea would take a change of clothes for all of us "girls:"
Barbara, Shirley, Carolyn, Mary Ann, Alice and me. Mine would be a
starched pinafore for sure.

I can see the men playing croquet on the manicured lawn with their
white shirts and straw hats on; the women would be drinking lemonade in
the shade and watching the children romping. Now I strive to follow the
same pattern with our "revived" Robertson reunion: the croquet, the
lemonade in an ancient cooler like Aunt Lizzie's, the genteel atmosphere,
etc.

Poppa always wore a hat and certainly on this special occasion he
made sure to have his very best one on.

Uncle Tom came by to drive Momma and Poppa to the reunion; he
mentioned something about Poppa's hat, but being too concerned with
situating the old ham in a safe spot on the floor, Poppa paid no attention.
When he got there, he discovered he had worn his old "everyday hat" and
his day was ruined! In complete disgust, he was heard to exclaim, "I look
just like Peter Goose!"

You remember Daddy killing the cat—something about lockjaw, selling eggs to Poppa, Hash's cinnamon rolls and brown sugar molasses. Then when we lived at Mommau's, you were stricken with rheumatic fever. We were all so upset; we had never had a major illness before. Wonder what happened to that old brown studio couch? That was the only couch Hash ever had for twenty years, wasn't it? You were all "laid out" on that couch, receiving visitors and accepting special privileges. Someone brought you a spectacular stack of "funny books." (We never called them "comic books" like most everyone else.) How delighted we all were—we read for months! Remember "Plastic Man"—how I admired his "reach."

During this time, you said you often dreamed you were afloat on the ocean in a tub. Rub-a-dub-dub—what a damp dream!

Hash and Mommau were both head-strong; how they lived together so long without real fire-works I don't understand. You say you remember Hash slamming doors there quite often; that is a "safe" way to let off steam.

Momma and Poppa had come for dinner when we lived "on the hill." That was an unusual occurrence because we always went to their house every Sunday and they rarely visited in return. I love to remember all the family coming in on Sundays; Momma and Bubble never seemed to mind at all, doing all that cooking. Aunt Mabel and Uncle Merdie, Jeanne and Tommy, Glenne and Bubby, Shelia and Charles, all of us, Uncle Pal and Auntie........a long forgotten way of life, the family gathering; now people don't want to be imposed on—we go out to eat—we see our families only occasionally and something is lost forever.

Much earlier, when Poppa was still alive and Momma did all the cooking herself, everyone would sit down to a huge meal in the long dining room at the house adjoining the store. I can see it—dimly. Sometimes, Momma cooked spare-ribs. Poppa said he loved to butcher a hog just so he could see "Fannie with grease on her chin."

After the meal, Momma would usually bring in a dessert; most often it would be one of her famous peach cobblers. Practically every time, Poppa would bang his fist on the table and bellow out: "Gosh ding it, Fannie, why didn't you tell me you had dessert so I wouldn't have eaten so much!"

However, this time they were at our house and the heating stove was going full blast in honor of the occasion. It was glowing red around the chimney and almost dancing with the heat. Something was wrong—Poppa opened the closet door behind it and started jerking clothes out—the attic was on fire! You were thrust up through that almost inaccessible opening, being the one small enough to put up and old enough to douse the flames. How highly excitable you were, especially that day but you did the job well, and again, you were the hero of the moment.

Moments of high excitement figured often in your life. There was the time you ran and grabbed a gun because there was a "wild animal" in the pantry. "Hash, I never saw anything like it—it has big eyes shining in the dark—I have to kill it before it eats the kids up." We were running and screaming from it, Hash was afraid for you to use the gun, but you were wild and you had to kill it—quick!! The deed was done—a light was shined on it—it was a little ole possum.........you ran screaming into the kitchen where Mommau was. It was night—there was no one in the house except the two of you—and a man was hiding in the corner, waiting to kill you both! But you were fearless and armed with an axe, so you advanced upon him in the dark room......Mommau came behind you and switched the light on just before you could completely demolish the coat rack in the corner where someone had recently hung an old overcoat and a sinister hat........You looked out the window during an electric storm, just as lightening ran down the tallest pine tree and into the clothes line, turning it bright red and making it dance violently. You jumped two feet off the floor and broke into a dead run through the house and where you would have stopped, no one knows, but Daddy managed to catch you as you streaked by, wild-eyed and out of breath. What times we had.

No matter what it was, to you it was always better if it was "snitched;" the unattainable and forbidden things were what you desired. Are you so much different today?

Mommau kept various delicacies in a suitcase under her bed. She left periodically and when she did she locked the door going into her room from our room. Before she was ever out of sight you would be pulling the little piece of thread that you had rigged up to lift the latch from the inside. You set it all up while the door was open—while she was still there!

Once, while Mommau was still there, we were all under her bed (again, I was only an innocent by-stander) eating grapefruit! Of course it was dark under the bed and since a boy always carried matches in his pocket, a little light on the subject would help matters. When the mattress began to scorch, our secret was divulged and you remember the rest!

Every boy needs a bike, so when there is no money for one, something else must be worked out. In one of your "funny books" you saw a "get rich quick" scheme and you immediately went into the business it advocated— selling Cloverine Salve! Soon you had everyone around Muddy Ford, Turkey Foot and Oxford believing they couldn't exist without a year's supply of the multi-purpose salve; it could, according to you, be used on everything.

It's uses ranged from a diaper ointment for Aunt Bea's new baby Carolyn to a cure-all for a bad leg on Cam Sutton's cow!

Soon you had your prized possession—the gleaming new bike and you were in your glory. Once, when you were doubling me, my heel caught in the spoke and I was dragged several feet along the road. All was well though, when I was taken to the house, and, you guessed it, rubbed down with Cloverine Salve! But I still have a great scar on my heel.

You were always a sucker for wild, far-out stories and schemes, as you still are at times. You fell completely for a story that a boy at school told you about a hidden treasure in Mammoth Cave. His name was Bobby Bowman and he convinced you that the key he had would open a hidden door at Mammoth Cave but that you could reach it only by means of a little boat. You were wild and eager to go claim the treasure, and I shared your frustration and anger when you failed to convince Daddy of the truthfulness of it. After all, he had nothing to lose if the treasure wasn't there, but he wouldn't even take you there to try!

It was the same frustration I felt when Daddy patiently and repeatedly explained to me the uselessness of me entering one of those word contests you still see in magazines today. He told me that, even though it was simple, an older more experienced person would more easily be able to figure out the words than I would, being only nine years old. But he didn't convince me either, and I bet you anything that treasure is still there in the murky waters, just waiting for that rusty key to turn in the lock..........

The fact that you always carried a thick roll of play money when we were little has carried over to your life now; you never let slip past you a chance to flash the ever-present roll of big bills you carry now—usually.

One thing I really regret is that I didn't play with you more often. Even though we played endless games of "cowboys" with you, at other times you would beg us to play and we didn't want to. Now when I hear Tracy asking Scarlett to play something with him, I take her aside and say: "go play with the 'little thing.' Soon he'll be too big and won't be begging you to play......." And she does. One day Shane wanted her to help him make a tent upstairs, and to my surprise she left something important she was doing and went with him. Over her shoulder she said to Alice and me, "He won't always be little and wanting me to play with him." What I said had made an impression!

The old smoke house was our back-drop then for the endless games of "cowboys" we played. A saloon was set up—coke was splashed into the little mugs and quickly downed by dusty throats—the safe was robbed repeatedly by desperados who galloped away on their stick horses through a cloud of dust. Our play money was not the fancy real-looking play money that kids like Shane have today—ours was painstakingly cut out of old magazines and catalogs. They were cut to the size of dollar bills and the different denominations were printed on by us. Somehow you always had the roll and you flashed it constantly.

But you and your money come to a parting of the ways very often, I hear. When you have it, you are at times very generous with it. Hash called to tell me about you swooping in upon her, full of open hearted generosity and giving her over a hundred dollars one day. How fine and good of you! And how like you to come back that night, as you did, and contritely borrow it back, after a run of "bad fortune." She laughed heartily at her "loss"—she had expected it.

I am still mad at you over that candy bar! If a girl can't have any privacy, what can she have?

My only privacy was my little jewelry box that I could lock and then carry the key on me at all times. I was proud to say you couldn't unlock it even with the many bobby pins you used on it.

I hid a candy bar in there, secure in the knowledge that it would be there when I went for it. How could I have been so foolish, thinking it was safe, actually leaving it in the same room with you; sometimes one never learns!

I knew something was wrong when I saw the pieces of colored wrapper shredded around the jewelry box. Then when I saw the chocolate on the bobby pin, the awful truth dawned on me—you had picked that candy bar out, bite by bite, through the tiny crack—with a bobby pin!

Memories, good and bad—there is no end to them, is there? We are blessed with our memories.

You were amazed at the fact that Hash finally got tired of hamburgers. She used to have an insatiable desire for hamburgers and cokes, but James would bring in unending pounds of hamburger for her and even though she sometimes had one for lunch everyday, she finally said she was tired of hamburger. I think you were just thankful that she was well taken care of in that way and had all she wanted to eat........

You say your fondest memories are of her dancing the Charleston..... reading the Bible and "preaching" to you........telling you that each day would take care of itself........

What I remember in regard to that is her surprise at the calm way you would sit and actually listen to her talking about the Bible, and this was recently—in the last few years.

I want you to know how much she appreciated the fact that you actually took the time to listen calmly to what she desperately wanted you to hear. This completely uncharacteristic behavior out of you really meant so much to her. I know, because she told me so.

# 16
# MARY ANN'S CHAPTER

Once, long ago, you and I were on Momma's front porch and we were all ready to leave for home. Hash and Daddy and the others walked toward the car, but before I left I had something I wanted to do. They all turned to watch when they heard me say, "Let me do something for *Maaary*." You were probably about two years old and you were sitting in the porch swing. I pushed the swing back as far and as high as I could, intending to give you one good last swing, but instead I dumped you out—"plop"—onto the hard floor. I did something for "Mary" alright and they all still remember it.

Well, what I am doing now, this book, I am doing for you all and I hope it will be appreciated more than what I did for you way back then.

You came into the picture on December 18, 1943 and were born at the John Graves Ford Memorial Hospital in Georgetown. We were living at the Cox Place at the time.

The name Mary came from Mary Alice, "Bubble," and the Ann from Aunt Ann. You were almost named Mary Lita, I have heard, but I don't know the story behind that.

An extremely early memory, one that I am able to place an age on, is when you were born and I stayed with Aunt Ann and Uncle Joe while Hash was in the hospital. That would make me two years old of course, and I remember it vividly. I had grown extremely attached to Uncle Joe during this short time and had even begun to call him "Daddy." When Hash and Daddy stopped at their house to get me on the way home, I clung to Uncle

Joe and cried. Can you imagine? I'd want to beat one of my children with a stick if they did that.

Speaking of beating your children reminds me of the occasion when Daddy tried to make you pick up a biscuit you had either dropped or thrown on the floor. He said it was the first and the last time he ever whipped you. The more he insisted that you pick it up, the more stubbornly you refused. I can't imagine such a thing and I wonder what came over you; we just never disobeyed Daddy—ever! There you were, as stubborn as a mule, absolutely refusing to pick it up, even though Daddy would give you another hard lick with the belt each time you refused.

I suppose you would both be still sitting there, locked in a battle of wills, with life passing on all around you, had not little Billy decided to act.

This is truly a classic story in our family and I love it. "Little ole' Bill," the silent spectator during all this commotion, summed up the situation and saw only one solution—disperse with the bone of contention, that being the biscuit—and both parties would win. Seizing the opportunity, he pounced upon the biscuit and did the only sensible thing—he ate it, thus breaking the deadlock.

I remember us all coming home from somewhere and going up the porch steps at the Cox Place, when a mean old rooster suddenly decided to attack. It "flopped" me—it "flopped" you—we were standing screaming with our hands and arms shielding our face. I don't know who ended the attack, probably Lowell went for the axe......

Another time, at the same house, you and I ran screaming for help—bumble bees were after us! Bumble bees were on us—everywhere! Hash pulled them frantically from our hair and never once got stung. Oh, we were wild that time, and if the truth be known, I bet Lowell was the one who stirred those bees up, don't you?

My memories don't come into clear focus on you until we lived in the little log house, and then there are no end to them.......the two of us sitting in front of the fire when we stayed with Mommau, pretending to comb our doll's hair, and marveling over the fact that "next month" we would be getting dolls with "real hair." Just imagine—real hair! We couldn't believe it nor could we wait—but we did, and they were well worth it. Also, at that time, Mommau would reach in that big wardrobe in the bedroom and give us both an old pocketbook of hers to play with. I can smell that old musky leather smell now and it all comes back to me.

One day Bubble came walking up through the yard and she had brought us both a dainty little doll dressed in a beautiful blue dress and a matching hat. They were too precious to be believed and I remember being absolutely enthralled! Bubble was unbelievably good to us all through our childhood and I appreciate her more all the time.

The wild cherry tree was truly our tree of dreams; there we spent many happy hours, sharing our dreams as well as our fears. We would perch in it's high branches, not unlike the twittering, flitting birds that called it home. Daddy always said we sounded like two magpies anyway, always whispering and giggling. In fact, he called us Heckle and Jeckle back then and in case you have forgotten, they were two birds of some sort.

You remember a black, stormy night at the log house when all the electricity went off and you said we children were all on the verge of being very much afraid.

Rising to the occasion, Hash lit a coal-oil lamp and gathered us all around her rocking chair. Then she proceeded to read some crazy story to us, presumably from a "funny book." You think it was a story about the "Sassin-bug," the one she never quit laughing about. When I would wear a big pair of sunglasses in later years, she would laugh and say I looked like a "Sassin-bug."

So as she read she got us all laughing and we became less aware of the storm raging outside.

In the same manner, you say you remember her gathering us all around her, like little hungry birds, as she would divide a bowl of corn flakes between us—poking a spoonful at one and then the other. She would pull the spoon back sometimes just before our mouth closed over it, and jokingly give it to the next in line. That was great fun and I remember it too.

Also, I remember a time that the car was broken down and while we waited for Daddy to go for help, she scared us half out of our wits with a story about werewolves. The fact that it was dark and rainy outside the car didn't help matters at all; I remember being absolutely scared to death.

I would go sit in her lap and my legs would hang down like an overgrown colt—I remember thinking that I would never consider myself too big to sit in her lap.

"They laughed when I sat down to play." Who else remembers that old advertisement that I believe concerned mail order piano lessons? For some strange, hidden reason in your mind, that slogan figures prominently in your memories of Hash. Let me know if you ever figure out the connection and what it is that gives you that wild, strange feeling. Is that the reason you started piano lessons a few years ago?

Our playhouses—what delights they were—to us! To the ordinary person who might wander into our little converted chicken house, it might seem quite insignificant, but that's because their eye could not appreciate the rows of discarded pots and pans and chipped jars. They of course could not be expected to discern the difference between the rich, dark smooth "garden dirt" that we delighted in for pies and the coarse reddish clay dirt which was perfect for cakes.

We had little baskets full of a long, straight weed which was green beans and one full of flat round leaves which was bread, but who else could know that? And when we picked a little basket full of the reddish purple poke berries, we knew they were inedible, but they did "can" so nicely in our little playhouse.

We played, literally, for hours and hours at a time and my fondest memories are of our sweet little playhouses. I regret so much that my kids never knew such simple delights and I used to dwell on it, until Alice, you set me straight on it. You simply said that, considering the way we are now and the things we have, there is simply no way possible for our kids to ever know how to entertain themselves in such a "primitive" way. Right she was.

We ran like wild young animals through the bushes and the brambles; we would swing from grapevines across creeks and rocks. I never cease to wonder how Hash could turn us loose like that and not worry.......

Water babies—what memories they evoke—little pink rubber babies to play with in the shallow creek or in the pond.

Now that we have swans on the lake at the farm, I am fascinated with them and I collect figurines and pictures of swans every chance I have. Bubble gave me a tiny white china swan she has had for years and when I got home, I shook something out of it and there was a "water baby." It brought back memories.

Hash once told me, in later years, how sad she was that she didn't go to school with you on your first day. Evidently you were the only one who cried when you had to go and she walked all the way down to Kay's with you, comforting you. But she just had on her robe, and if she had gotten ready first, she could have ridden to school with you and Kay for the short time the first day lasted. I don't know why that bothered her so, but she mentioned it to me not too many years ago.

I can remember going off to school from Mommau's house, waiting on the front porch for the bus to pop over the hill. I had on that hooded raincoat that later burned in the fire, and I made silly faces at you as you pressed your nose against the window from inside.

Why did you slowly and deliberately and sadistically eat away at my little marshmallow man? Why? I painstakingly made him at school from marshmallows and raisins and toothpicks and sundry other things; I meant for him to last, as all my things did. But every day when I would come home from school, you had nibbled another raisin or a piece of marshmallow and it would make me cry. And the way Hash acted—she even seemed to be trying to keep from laughing and she looked as guilty as you did. I'll never forgive you for that!

Just before you were born, Hash and several others all stopped by Aunt Ann's house on the way to the hospital. There they played the piano and sang some songs and Hash proved her agility in the very face of childbirth by kicking her leg high over a chair! Wasn't she a character?

Speaking of Aunt Ann and your birth, she was around for mine too.

Let her tell you about it sometimes. Aunt Ann and Uncle Joe were always good to us—Hash thought a lot of both of them.

When I used to stay all night with them, Virginia would let me get in her closet where she had the most fabulous collection of dolls and they were the dolls she had played with when she was my age and I was overwhelmed with them.

I would watch Virginia roll her bangs at night and wish I was her age. When we were kids, we always thought the next age would be better, didn't we, but actually each year has it's charms.

You are undoubtedly the one most like Hash; you, of the many shifts of moods from extreme high to the very lowest. You can seldom ever hit a happy medium, can you? Perhaps you would miss the extremes if you ever did. Your temperment, your sensitive emotions, so easily hurt, and even the texture of your skin is identical to hers.

At first glance, you were like none of us; you don't look at all like the other four of us. We all are alike in looks—Daddy marked us, that's for sure. Because of your being so different, Lowell labeled you the "black sheep." That title, applied to you, has always delighted me. He, of course, is the classic black sheep, but his bestowing of the title on you I find absolutely hilarious!

"Here we go off to the tomato patch, the tomato patch, the tomato patch......." How I wish I could remember the rest of the words about the dusty feet on the path, carrying a bucket between us. We were as happy and carefree as two little girls could possibly be. Hash gave us the job of going after the tomatoes at the garden, so we made a game and a song out of it. I can recall exactly how the fine dust sifted through our toes as we skipped merrily along.

Kay sent you to her garden to pick some lettuce for lunch—you came back with a basketfull of tobacco plants!

I've always admired Kay for her great sense of humor; she is always ready for a good laugh and this time was no exception. She laughed loud and long and did without the lettuce for lunch.

For some reason, we both seemed to enjoy ministering to old women. We would put several trays of ice cubes in a jar and walk down to see Mary Barnhill. She wasn't really an old woman, but to us she seemed like one. She always seemed appreciative of the ice; she would dump it into her water bucket immediately and then she would show us all her flowers in the yard and the little musical instrument in the corner. I believe it was a mandolin.

Next, we would go down to see Miss Alice Shirley. Little Miss Alice, with her thin body bent almost double. She was indeed old—how old I don't recall. We would sit in her dim little room and she would bring out her picture postcards for us to view through her stereoscope. We never tired of doing that—time after time. Then we would read the Bible to her and offer to sweep the floor or go get her groceries. She was sweet and she appreciated our little visits.

Tumbling into bed together each night, we would both try to say these very important words first: "Scratch my back and tell me a story!" The one who succeeded would be the recipient of both delights.

You believed everything I ever told you. You looked at me for the answers—right or wrong. I tried to give them to you straight. At one time we were hearing so much talk about the Communists taking over that you came asking me what that would mean for us. Drawing on my great storehouse of wisdom, I explained that if such a thing did happen, it would mean that the Communists would get one-half of everything we might have. To better help you grasp the meaning, I used an illustration of a chicken—one-half for them—one-half for us. Just recently you told me that you took that literally, as the gospel truth, and kept waiting to hear the news about dividing up the chickens.

I would sit out in the swing and sing a certain song over and over because you begged me to. It was a song called "I Really Don't Want to Know." What a fabulous singer I must have been.

We played a game of blindfolding each other and taking as many steps as the other told us to; you led me to the edge of the rock wall and told me to take two steps. I did, and crumpled to a heap on the hard ground. Small wonder that I vowed to never trust you ever again. Your lame excuse was, "I thought you would stop when you didn't feel any ground under your feet!"

It was fall of the year—the tree hung heavy with pears. As little Mary viewed the ripe excess, she had a bright idea: she would gather one pear for each member of the family and put them away until winter. How delicious they would be then and how everyone would brag on Little Mary! Laboriously she worked: choosing only the most perfect ones and carefully wrapping them in newspaper. Then came the most important decision of all—where would she hide them?

Why, you ask, would she even hide them? Because, a hungry predator spelled L-O-W-E-L-L walked the grounds, his evil eyes always searching for something edible. No crack or crevice was considered secret; no small delicacy could you call your own. Cunningly, Little Mary chose a day when "he" was gone. Her deed was done in secret; she dared tell no one lest her secret be divulged. She hid them in a small box in a large box in a sack under some paper in a corner of the old safe in the dark corner of the smokehouse. When she was all alone. Unseen.

She smiled secretly to herself as she waited and anticipated the family's delight. A week passed and then two; maybe she wouldn't wait till winter. Maybe the time was ripe now—as ripe as the golden pears. She scurried to the smokehouse, unable to contain herself any longer and opened the safe back in the corner and took the little box out of the big box out of the sack out from under the paper in the back corner.

Alas! And alack also! The pears were gone! The predator had struck again!

Now it was winter. Every man for himself. The predator was running scared—snacks were scarce. The closest thing he had had to a delicacy for two weeks was snow cream; what was a boy to do?

Poor little Mary had happened upon an orange. From where I do not know; maybe it fell from heaven. As usual, she wanted to save for a "special" occasion. That was her downfall. After "he" left for the day, she built a snowman. A nice big fat snowman. A snowman with a secret—an orange right smack down in the middle of him. Safe and hidden.

Daddy and L-O-W-E-L-L came home and started up the walk to the house. Without ever breaking his stride, and with only one deft movement of his hand Lowell performed a swift "Orangeadectomy" on that poor snowman. Absolutely unbelievable!

Why is it so painful for you to look back? Can your memories be so different from mine? Surely not, but why is it? I try to talk to you and make you remember but you remember very little. You have put up a wall and I wonder why.

You say the immediate picture that comes to mind when you think of Hash is one of her smiling and sitting on the couch—reading and watching TV. You said she would jump up when you came in, anxious to see what she could do for you, and not what you could do for her. She always wanted to fix you something good to eat. Is that why we always equate food with hospitality?

Your fondest memories are of the "good" care she gave you when you were sick—holding your head and covering you with blankets she had warmed before the fire. Warm, loving memories of a mother's tender care.......

You and I were in the front yard playing. Hash came out to tell you she wanted to cut you some "bangs." Startled and wild-eyed, you asked, "What's bangs?" (What's a milkshake?) You soon found out as she deftly manipulated those scissors across your forehead—leaving you with a real set of bangs—a little more than an inch long!

Evidently you recovered from the shock and liked the bangs, because you stuck with them for years to come. Remember how our school pictures revealed and magnified every flaw our hair might have—bangs that were shaggy or even worse—much too short!

Momma would rather to have teased you than anything in the world; she loved to see you get mad. She would say something about those big cow-eyes and you would just have a "fit." Then she would laugh and laugh, calling you a little "spit-fire." I loved that nickname.

You came in with a dress that was old fashioned; it was different than any you had ever worn. Momma called you "Pearlie May" and that name stuck, didn't it? Bubble still calls you that occasionally.

"There's something so stylish about you, Anne." That quotation from one of her "Anne of Green Gables" books was always applied to you and I loved to hear her tell you that—it sounded so "fancy."

"Tempest and Sunshine." Remember that book? I found it in an antique store one day and bought it for old time's sake. That title fitted us exactly, didn't it? How did we ever get along so famously through all those childhood years, being so different? But get along we did, and in a wonderful way. That's why my childhood memories are all so good—I had you to share them with. Thanks for the memories!

That's one thing I regret about Alice—she had to grow up without a sister close to her age. Now that we are grown, the years between us have melted away, but in those important formative years, she had no one.

How Hash loved to hear from you and you called her often. I don't believe you wrote too much, but that didn't matter—she hated letters. I never heard of a person hating letters, but she did, because, as she said, "It meant she was expected to write one in return." Do you know of her ever writing a letter? Her script resembled a chicken's scratching; how did we ever develop such beautiful penmanship?

In her billfold you found something that really told the story on her; it was a little book of stamps and to show how long it had been since she had used them—they were nine cent stamps!

So Mary, don't be afraid to look back; look back and smile. Remember all the good things, and most of all—remember that you often said: "I love you Hash."

# 17
# BILLY'S CHAPTER

"Oh, my lit-tle bunny rat, oh, my lit-tle bunny rat." Who ever heard of a bunny rat??

My immediate picture of you as a child is one of you out riding your little tricycle and singing the above song to yourself. Over and over.

You were little and cute and "chunky" and we would all peep out the window and laugh at you as you went about your business of playing, oblivious of us.

We were all older than you and Alice hadn't come along so as we roamed over the hills and dales, you stuck close to Hash and the little tricycle; that was your security.

Hash was thirty years old when you were born and Daddy was thirty-one. He was cutting tobacco for Willy Morris when you arrived in Lexington at the Good Samaritan Hospital on September 19, 1945. It was about 9:00 o'clock in the morning and I'll bet that was one of the earliest things you ever did!

Dr. Taylor delivered you but Hash almost rejected you when you contacted that dreadful rash, impetigo, while still in the hospital.

However, she was finally persuaded to bring you on home. There was a dainty bassinett awaiting you at Bubble's, trimmed in blue satin ribbons, but before you, could be deposited in it, Vonnie, who was just a baby himself, climbed over into it somehow and promptly fell fast asleep. That would have been alright, except when he was discovered it was also discovered that he was as muddy as a little pig!

You were brought home to the Cox Place where we lived for but a short while longer before moving to be with Mommau, following Poppau's death on November 2.

Remember how the old patriarch's used to bless the newborn babies by holding them in their arms and raising them upward? That's the picture I always had of Poppau and you; you were taken in to him as he lay in bed and even though he held you in his arms, I'm sure he was too weak to raise you up......

Mommau would sit and "nuss" you on the porch with her apron wrapped around you; you helped to fill her void of emptiness after Poppau's death. But she lamented: "Just as I get used to having him, you'll take him away."

She spoiled and pampered you and I guess we were jealous because I remember teasing you unmercifully over a song she sang to you. It was "Yankee Doodle Dandy" and after she would sing the part to you about Yankee Doodle going to town on a "pacing" pony we would take you aside and sing you our version. We called it a "pissin'" pony and you would just have a "fit."

There is a little scene I can vaguely see played out in my mind: There are several of us, possibly Mary and Lowell and me, pulling a little wagon with a baby on a pillow, around and around through the house. At first we go fast, but then we gradually pull it slower and slower because the baby is going to sleep. When that feat is accomplished, we quietly park the wagon in a corner and Hash is so pleased........

Recently Tracy pulled me through the house, around and around, in his little wagon and I laid there with my eyes closed and tried to recapture the exact feeling of it all, but it never came clearly to my mind......it was blurry as if the memory was encased in velvet......Dr. Stoll says that if you can ever recapture the exact feeling that you had in one of your earliest memories, you have made contact with your very essence, your very core. He says that essence remains the same—you are always the same all through the years and that part of you never ever changes.

You remember us all being away at school and you were at home alone—you and Hash. But then it was permissible for the little brothers and sisters to go off to school with the older ones whenever they had the urge. Isn't that funny? You went with us several times and being so amiable and cute, you were always welcomed by the teachers. Of course, the fact that Kay and Aunt Ann were both teaching then helped a lot.

One day they were taking class pictures so we took you along to be included. Hash dressed you up in a little camel sports jacket and slicked your hair back and you grinned broadly for the camera. But the main thing I remember about the picture, which is my favorite one of you, is the happy little dandelion we picked as we walked to school and stuck in your buttonhole! Isn't that absolutely priceless—it makes me happy to remember such things!

You "grinned" all the time back then and everyone "grinned" back at you; it was contagious. When Daddy would take you to the store with him, all the men who congregated there would bribe you with pennies and nickels to "shake" for them. Surely you can remember "shaking." You would stand stiff and still, with your hands in your pockets, moving nothing except your legs, but they would be vibrating as if by an electric motor. To the best of my knowledge it was the off-shoot of some dance step you had seen on Uncle Tom's television, and it was your claim to fame!

Even in the coldest winter time, you had an aversion to shoes. Shedding them at every opportunity got you in trouble with Daddy; he finally said he was going to whip you with a belt if he caught you barefooted one more time!

You say you remember sitting on the couch, gloriously barefooted and oblivious to the threat of frostbite, when Daddy unexpectedly walked in. They couldn't catch you with a fly net—you scattered in every direction. Hash had scared you "into your shoes" on numerous occasions by saying "Here comes your Daddy." But that finally lost its effect because she was only bluffing, but finally he did catch you.

Speaking of bare feet reminds me of how terrified Scarlett was one day when I mentioned her bare feet. Being only two years old or so, she hadn't heard the expression and I can still see the horror on her little face as she looked down to see if she really had "*bear* feet!!"

No sooner had I cleared up that little expression until I shocked her again, badly. Imagine her consternation when she overheard me tell Gadie, "Scarlett is a little hoarse (horse) this morning!" We had to pick her up off the floor after that one! She has always been one to take things literally!

Even though there are many advantages to being the "littlest kid," which you were until Alice came along, being the last one to take a bath in an old wooden tub outside is definitely not one of them. You didn't relish that at all, and did everything you could to get out of it. One fine day you took to flight as Hash was trying to catch you; it was "your turn." Running over the hill like the little "Gingerbread Man," you looked back over your shoulder to see if Hash was gaining on you and ran smack into the fox's mouth—Daddy's arms in this case! Hoisting you up over his shoulder, he carried you back up the hill and dumped you unceremoniously into the scummy water. A boy just didn't have a chance back in those days.

Hash used to scare us all the time; perhaps that's what's wrong with us—I mean, with the rest of you.

She used to stick her finger through that hole in the kitchen door of the old cabin while hiding in the darkness on the other side. Now there is something about a disembodied finger or eye that can really make a child come unglued and we were no exception.

Can any of us forget that traumatic experience at the old fallen down corn crib "up the holler?" We were playing inside it, having a fine time and minding our own business. It was at least one half mile away from the house, but we never had any reason to be scared back then.

Part way through our game, an uneasy silence fell upon us; we sensed that something was wrong. The hair raised up on the back of my neck and I realized that we were being watched—but by what? Drawn as if by a magnet, my reluctant eyes slowly traveled up the side of the crib wall to lock into the evil gaze of one large watery pale blue eye, framed by a peep-hole in the wood!

For several numbing seconds that cold blue eye held us transfixed until by sheer terror our spell was broken as we all tumbled pell-mell out of the high crib onto the ground and ran for our life, screaming at the top of our lungs.

But someone—I believe it was little Mary—made the mistake of looking back, like Lot's wife, and saw you standing with outstretched arms and a distorted face in the window of the corncrib. We had forgotten you! But how could we go back? That evil disembodied eye was still lurking behind it, but "little ole' Bill" was depending on us. Back we went with a dreadful trepidation, jerked you out of the window, and ran like—well, you remember the rest. Risking one more backward glance we saw *Daddy* step out from behind the corncrib and we experienced the full gamut of emotions, beginning with relief, anger, disbelief, amazement and ending with an overwhelming desire to do something dreadful to Daddy? How we have laughed as we remembered that incident over the years.

**Being too young to differentiate between masculine and feminine** pursuits, you happily accompanied Hash to the monthly "Homemaker" meetings. You were awakened to the "difference" by Daddy and Lowell's teasing remarks about buying you a little dress to wear from then on. I imagine that was the last time you went.

Hash would miss you at times, but she wouldn't get alarmed. She would just put her book down and send one of us down to see if you had wandered off to Mrs. Drake's house again. There we would find you as we had expected, pulled up to the table in a little chair and having dinner with Mrs. Drake.

But at other times, Hash would send you down to Kay's on some little errand and about an hour later, she would send one of us down to find you. There you would be, dawdling beside the lane, totally engrossed in whatever had caught your attention—a "tumblin' bug," a grasshopper or maybe a little bird with a broken wing. Without fail, you had completely forgotten what your initial mission had been, but no one cared; nothing was ever a life or death matter back then anyway........Now when Cheryl does the same thing, Kay just laughs and overlooks it because she too remembers........

I remember the time Aunt Mabel took it upon herself to cut your hair and how "mad" Daddy was when he saw how much cutting she had to do to "even it up."

I remember us all running through the plowed field in front of the cabin; it was muddy and we were barefooted and our feet got so heavy with the accumulated mud we could barely move. What fun!

I remember the hot tar that had been poured on the road in front of Mommau's house and how we all walked through it barefooted (after it cooled) and mashed the bubbles with our toes. Oh, the simply joys of a country childhood—what can compare to them? I'm truly thankful we grew up as we did—in the country.

You say you remember Hash getting mad about being "stuck up that holler" and "striking out" for Momma's or anywhere just to get away. You were "stringing" along behind her of course, trying to keep up with your fat little legs.

I remember a late spring Sunday when we were all going out to fly kites in a field near Kay's house, but first I wanted to finish dusting the furniture. So often now, my Sundays feel like that Sunday of long ago.........

Once you did some mischievous thing (and weren't you and Vonnie the masters of mischief back then?) and Bubble snapped: "If you were mine, I'd spank you!" Looking her right in the eye, you answered sweetly, "that's why I'm glad I'm not yours."

You loved Hopalong Cassidy and I loved Roy Rogers. We argued incessantly over who was the bravest, who could shoot the fastest and which one had the better horse; I made cruel jokes about the name Hopalong and you ridiculed "Old Squint Eyes."

We never wavered in our loyalty to our favorite though, and through the years I kept up with Roy. We even went to a Rodeo to see him and do you know, he even shook hands with my little Scarlett! What did old "Hoppy" ever do for you?

Roy even joined me in teasing you about Hopalong's name—remember that song not so long ago that Roy sang called, "Hoppy, Gene (Autry) and Me?"

Last month I read a little article in the newspaper about Roy deciding to sell off all his horses because they were becoming too much of an expense. Now, what I love about Gadie is his willingness to go along with some of my wilder ideas as if they were quite normal, and in no time at all I had gotten the phone number of "Apple Valley" in California and was asking to speak to Roy Rogers! Alas, he was out and the secretary told us the horses had been sold a few days earlier. Otherwise, Gadie said we just might have flown down to consider buying one, just because they were his. He likes Roy too.

Mary and I used to catch you after you had been tormenting and teasing us about something or the other and while one of us held you down, the other would wash your face with an old greasy dish rag. A dish rag that may have washed dishes after a meal of liver and onions. A dish rag that was not only greasy, but *cold* and greasy. And we scrubbed you down good.

Even though your next move was always the same, the very predictableness of it made it no less infuriating. After breaking loose from our grip, you would run as fast as your legs would carry you, never breaking stride until you reached our dresser drawers and thereupon you would dump the entire contents of them on the floor. Never have I seen anyone derive such satisfaction from one vengeful act. Time after time you retaliated in that "childish" way and each time left Mary and me more frustrated than the time before.

Often little boys are unappreciated despite all their efforts to the contrary; such was the time you "outdid" yourself in trying to help us set up a new playhouse. Carolyn was there and we ran you back and forth with requests for this and that and you never once complained. After you had us all set up and all our demands had been met, we were ready to play. Then Carolyn disdainfully asked: "What's he doing in here? I wish he'd leave!" Poor little boys just don't have a chance around a bunch of girls!

It was different with Lowell; he included you in all our escapades and made you a part of things. Once he came up with the most elaborate scheme and we all played a part in it. We laid blankets on the floor of that old attic room of the cabin. Then, because he convinced us that someone would surely try to sneak up the steps during the night and kill us all in our sleep, he tied a string to the front door downstairs, all the way through the house, and back up the stairs. Then we all had the string tied to each of our hands so we could signal when danger was near. None of us closed an eye all night—except Lowell.

You were into gourmet food quite early if froglegs qualify as gourmet food. You and Mary, upon gigging a few hapless frogs in a little pond at Mommau's place would go into the barn and build a fire. There you would cook the froglegs in a little pan brought along just for the occasion. Now the gigging and the cooking was a fine thing to do, but *in* the barn? It's a great wonder it was still standing when your culinary efforts were finished!

You were always smart; not only common-sense smart, but scholastically smart. I've always admired your intelligence and I remember telling Scarlett and Tracy that I believe you could give them an answer to any question they ask—not to trick questions, but factual answers to such advanced subjects as the workings of the universe and the chemistry of life and the makeup of an atom, etc. You understand those things; that's the way your mind runs.

Not me; my mind runs to the dreamy side of life—thoughts and impressions and ideas all merging vaguely together as if in a thin water color picture; a picture that I can enjoy and understand but one that others might view and shake their heads in derision........

Should you use your intelligence in an intelligent way and extend yourself to the right degree, there is no way of knowing what you could accomplish. I'd love to see it.

Many lively discussions of the Bible were shared between you and Hash and she entered into them wholeheartedly, perhaps at times exasperating you with her pertinacity.

You held your own, but she had the advantage over you because while you could quote many scriptures, you didn't have her keen knowledge of where they were located in the Bible. There she had the edge on you, and didn't she know it? She could flip through that little worn Bible of hers and find any subject in a snap; here she was in her element and in full command.

Your style differed. You parried back and forth with her, presenting your views as in a phantasmagoria; she, armed with the facts and nothing but the facts, Mam, was straight forward and sure of herself. Once you complimented her with these apt words: "I guess you know that you know more about the Bible than anyone I've ever talked to." Yes, she knew. Indeed she knew.

You remember the year we ate all the popcorn. You say you had no real resentment about the divorce case, even though you remember being "mad" at both of them. And do you remember her rolls?

Do memories make things better for you or worse? People differ. Certain things make the whole thing better for me and they are just strange litle things. When I see the tulips around her grave readying themselves to bloom, as they are now, and hear all the birds sing, I feel a special calmness. In some odd way I even feel like things are alright again. And two days from today it will be April 8.

"Riddle—ma—riddle—ma—riddle—mar—ree. What could you see that we couldn't see?" I don't really know if you actually saw things we never saw or if you just put such a different interpretation on the ordinary things that they appeared different. Whatever the case, you view life at a differing angle than the rest of us; you flip to a distant flute!

Once, in exasperation but only half-seriously, Hash dismissed some of your far-out ideas with these final words: "You're possessed."

Thankfully, that's not true, but one could come to such a conclusion after hearing some of your more advanced theories served with perhaps a dash of dipsomania!

I could never imagine you being anything but kind and respectful to Hash and isn't that a fine thing to remember? Just think how much she appreciated those qualities in you.

You were standing beside her hospital bed, you and Lowell, after hearing the doctor say that it did indeed look like she was dying....You were looking down at her, surely trying to conceal your emotions, when she opened her eyes and saw you there. Reaching out and taking you both by the hand, she smiled sweetly and said, "My boys." Just that—"My boys." No big emotional outburst, no climactic scene—none of that was her style. All her life she had been herself, straight-forward and simple; why should she change now?

And now, the end was near and once again you were her little boy,
amusing her with some nonsensical ditty. I didn't hear this myself, but
someone walked in on a private moment you were sharing with her and
heard you singing "some funny little song" to her. I'm quite sure it was:
"Oh, My lit-tle bunny rat, oh, my lit-tle bunny rat" because they told me
how Hash was smiling........

# 18
# ALICE'S CHAPTER

Alice, the poor motherless child; that's the way I think of you in relation to her death. You needed her more than any of us—your loss was probably greater. You, being her "baby," held a very special place in her heart. I know she worried about you a lot, as mothers often do.

She was thirty-five when you were born; I wonder if she knew you would be the last. Being born on July 13, 1949, you were her only "summer baby." You were born at 10:35 in the morning at John Graves Ford Memorial Hospital here in Georgetown and delivered by Dr. Wilt.

Mary Ann and I were absolutely thrilled to have you. I wonder if we helped Hash much; I can't even remember changing your diaper. I'm sure we entertained you constantly though, and that would have been a help.

Hash was happy and relaxed after you were born and she looked good. There is a picture of her holding you outside the hospital, before she started home. She still kept her style and fashionable ways, even immediately after a birth, because she had on a black suit and a hat with a feather in it! Can you imagine any of us dressing up like that to leave the hospital? We would squeeze back into the maternity dress we came in or wear a new robe perhaps. But not Hash—she had a lot of pride!

Your earliest memory is of Hash curled up on the couch where we lived with Mommau—reading a book! How strange. I too remember about you and Hash's books. Naturally you didn't like to see her reading when you wanted her attention so you did what any smart child would do—you hid her books. Every time her book was "misplaced," she would laugh, knowing who the culprit was.

You remember her fixing you a great big chocolate homemade cake and telling you about a little black lamb. Lambs figure very significantly in my memories too. There was something very special to her about lambs.

It was very seldom that she went to town; it was very seldom that she had any extra money when she went to town. But on a few occasions, I can fondly recall her bringing us little white chalk lambs to play with. She got them at the "Ten Cent Store" and we were delighted with them. I believe she brought them to us several times and I can also remember white bunnies with pink ears—some of them were standing up and some were sitting.

Then you got sick, terribly sick, and she almost lost you. You were about nine months old and you evidently developed Spinal Meningitis. Bubble came to our house and as soon as she saw you, she knew you were deathly sick. Your fever was so high your diaper would immediately dry on you after you wet. Now that's what I call a high fever!

On the way to the hospital, Bubble said you gave her a little weak smile, and Mary Ann commented: "Now we can't see her make anymore of those funny little faces."

After keeping you under an oxygen tent for several days, you seemed to show improvement, so it was removed and taken from the room. Daddy was watching you closely, so when you began gasping for breath he grabbed you up only to feel you go completely limp on his shoulder. The nurse, who happened to be a relative of ours, Irene Morris, ran for Dr. Wilt who immediately tapped your spine with a needle and that evidently saved your life. But still they thought you were dying and Hash, unable to bear the pain and sorrow of seeing you die, made someone take her home to Momma's house. There she fled to her old room upstairs and almost went insane!

Billy, being the only child there, supposedly, and only four years old, witnessed the whole scene. In relating it to me recently, his words to describe the whole ordeal was that it was "very heavy." Hash ran from one bed to the other, crying and praying and vowing never to smoke again, if only God would let her baby live.........

She must surely have thought about her own mother losing little Gertie Lee at eleven months; she would have remembered hearing about the agony Momma went through, reaching in the night for a baby that was no longer there........and little Chester, her brother, had died at age thirteen.

Someone came with word that you were alive, that indeed you were even improving, but Hash at first refused to go, thinking they wanted her there only to tell her you were dead. Finally she went and rejoiced with Daddy, who had never left, that not only were you alive, but that the crisis and the fever had passed. Earlier, Daddy had been waiting in the hall and only when he heard your cry did he too know you had survived.

She never did smoke again either; she was not one to take an oath lightly. I can remember her chewing gum and eating ice constantly to take the place of the cigarettes.

After that you had no more troubles; you fell into line with the rest of us, but being in the unenviable position of being "the youngest" didn't set too well with you. I remember you pouting quite a lot because Mary Ann and I were "too grown up" to want to play your little games and Billy was too rough. What's a kid to do?

Who can forget that picture of you coming up the front yard, riding a stick horse and wearing a little fringed cowgirl outfit—and a terrible scowl! You were about six years old and no one would play cowboys with you.

A cowgirl needs a pony—then she can do without playmates or anything else! What a fabulous dream—to have a pony.!

One magical day Daddy came in with a pony for you; it was a marvelous little pony and you could ride it all by yourself! Howard Stephens let Daddy have it for the day and you were in "seventh heaven." Good ole' Howard, I like him so well. He's a good, generous man and I've always thought so much of him. When we had a carnival at Garth School and I was in charge of getting some ponies for rides, I called and asked him if he had any to loan out, and indeed he did. He even gave them free of charge and made the carnival a huge success. I appreciated that so much.

Daddy came leading the pony up the road for you and immediately four conniving minds began to work: How could we get that pony away from you? After all, it was the first real live pony we had ever had too. Of course there had been "Ole' Charlie," and Kay had Bess and Nickel; we rode them all the time. Once Mary and I were on Nickel and that horse walked right into the creek and started pawing water as hard as it could. There was nothing we could do except sit there and get soaked.

But that pony was a different story and we all had aims on it. Now almost twenty-five years later, I sincerely hope you will accept my sincere apology for what Mary and I did. We talked you into letting us have one little ole' short ride, and just like it was when Mary kept picking and picking away at my little marshmallow man, there was no way we could stop. We just couldn't bring ourself to turn it around and so we kept going straight ahead—all the way to Momma's—two and a half miles away! In the meantime you kept watching for us to come back over that hill until gradually the awful truth dawned on you—we weren't coming back—at least not right away.

Subsequently, you did what any "livid" five year old would do—you started after us as fast as your little short legs would carry you. When we saw you coming we realized the full extent of what we had done: Two big long-legged girls riding off with our little baby sister's "treat" for one day. We felt as low as any two horse thieves ever felt, and guess who walked all the way home?

Then to top it all off, Billy somehow got on the pony later and was gone for about an hour! What's a cowgirl to do?

Bubble came one day and we all went paw-paw hunting. Hash looked around and realized there was no little Alice so we all trekked back to where we had started from and there you stood, waiting patiently. After all, it wasn't the first time you had been left........after searching for you for quite some time on another occasion, you were finally located standing forlornly in the middle of the tobacco patch, where the stalks were several feet higher than you were!

Scarlett has been riding horses since she was about four years old and I have a priceless movie of her with a long gown on and her hair flowing way down her back like "Baby Godiva." She was on big while Jubilee, (I wanted to name the farm "Jubilee Place" because that was our first horse.) and she looked like a little horse fly. As she grew older, her horses improved and after Jubilee and Baldy there was Gypsie, and now April is the current horse.

Seeing her on that horse when she was so tiny reminded me of your riding a big horse bareback when you were about that same age. It was out in the field at Mommau's and Daddy was so proud; you clung on that big broad back like you were an experienced horsewoman.

Then at the farm about six years ago you started to get up on a pony when your boot hit against the trash can. It startled the pony and it almost ran out from under you, leaving you sitting on the rump and clinging to the back of the saddle while the pony ran full speed ahead. It was the funniest sight imaginable; you looked like that old drunk in the movie "Cat Ballou." We were laughing so hard we almost died, but I finally managed to stop the pony and disengage you.

But of my memories of you and horses, my favorite is of the wild races we used to have on Jubilee and Baldy in the field beside our house in town. It was when Scarlett was about six or seven. We would start on one end of the field and race as hard as we could go to the other end, all the time screaming and hollering like crazy women! That was the most exhilarating thing I can ever remember doing—those hooves thundering and nostrils flaring—and I was scared to death! But we did it over and over and over once we started; we were never ones for moderation, were we?

Who did we call "Ole' Money Bags"—was it you or Mary? Mommau gave one of you a handful of change and you tied it up in a handkerchief and got it out every hour or so to count it. I believe it was you.

I feel sorry about your childhood though and I feel you were really left sadly behind us as we grew up ahead of you and never really took the time to look back to see how you were doing or if you needed help........There must have been many times you did need help—a little lonely figure with a pixie haircut—cheated of many things.

Before you started to school, you would go down to Momma's, sit down in the ever present red rocking chair, cross your little short legs and say to Momma: "Well, tell me all you know." Momma loved that—you were a little ole' woman who came to "set a spell" and hear the latest gossip.

Mary Ann and I would actually take you out where Hash couldn't hear us and tell you we were going to have to spank you just so we could see you "drop your lip." When you would do it we would hug you and tell you we were just kidding—then we would proceed to do it all over again. How sadistic of us!

You had your moments though, being the youngest. When we would return home at night, the few nights we went out, we all had to trudge up the lane to our little cabin behind Kay's house.

There's nothing much worse than going to sleep in the car (or truck) and having to wake up and walk on a freezing cold night another half a mile or so. Hash used to say we looked like a mule train coming through there—that song was popular at the time. But you, being the "little squirt" of the family, got carried by Daddy! How I envied you then!

Speaking of songs that were popular then reminds me of how scared and excited I felt one dark night when Lowell and I had to walk past Kay's barn by ourselves; he had to start talking about those "Night Riders in the Sky" and those big black clouds looked so much like them, rolling along........

Remember the night Daddy brought home a real live monkey for you and it was sitting there on the dresser, just waiting for some little kid like you to come and start playing with it? You were so excited you could hardly contain yourself and just about to burst but everyone else was asleep so you just laid there in bed and watched it until morning. With the stark morning light came the awful realization that your "monkey" was only a paper sack cruelly contorted into that magical shape by a little girl's imagination........ Does this story belong in Mary Ann's chapter? It may have been Mary Ann instead of you.

Aunt Mabel always brought fancy little Easter baskets to everyone of us when we all congregated at Momma's; we would be wearing the cute little straw bonnets Kay bought us. Then we would put on coats and go out in the cold damp grass and look for eggs, freezing.

Lazy Liza Lizard. How do you feel when you hear the title of that little book? There seemed to be something special about that story; Hash loved to tell you about it or read it to you.

One night in the log cabin when you were small, we had some lively music on the radio. Daddy wasn't there and we all, including Hash, danced around and around, twirling in gay abandon, faster and faster until we all finally collapsed in exhaustion. I remember thinking how much fun it was and why hadn't we done it before and surely we would do that every night from then on!

Then came your turn to start to school and it is said that you cried every day. What's a school girl to do? I suppose you finally adjusted to it, as we do to most situations if given time enough.

Then came that sad night when Daddy called us all around him in front of the stove and as we waited to hear, not what he would say, but how he would say it, our concern was for you alone, because the rest of us already knew that Hash would never be calling that house on the hill "home" again. Until that week, Daddy had hopes that she would, but when he finally realized that it was all over between them, he took you on his knee and told you that "Hash wouldn't be coming back."

What a traumatic experience that must have been; indeed you cried like your heart would break and I took you in another room to comfort you and to tell you that even though she wouldn't be coming back, you would be going to where she was.

Thus began your transition from one life to another at the impressionable age of eight, and sadly enough, somewhere along the way you found yourself cheated out, not only of a father, but even of a father figure.

But you survived and grew. You spent a lot of time at our house; you got off the school bus most days at my house and waited for Hash and James to pick you up. You would eat orange sherbet and then I would send you to the store to get honeybuns for me. I'm sure you remember!

When you moved to Etta Lane with Hash and James, you inherited a job—feeding the hogs Gadie had on a "pig farm" a short distance down the road. You seemed to enjoy feeding and watering them and washing down the concrete and it was the greatest help to Gadie.

Back then money was "scarce" for us; it was practically nonexistent. However, Gadie appreciated so immensely the help you were to him that in one fine munificent moment, he bought you a shining new English bicycle! This was with the only fifty dollars he had to his name!

Now you were growing up and big Mary took you aside to give you some sisterly advice on how to dress and act. Somewhere in the conversation she cautioned you against wearing too much makeup and advocated the idea of allowing your natural look to shine through. You slowly looked her over, allowing your amused eyes to come to rest on her head of newly dyed, firey red hair and your caustic reply: "Good ole' natural Mary" is another classic we remember often!

Hash was sentimental and after you and Butch married, she missed you. Having been in the habit of opening your door every morning and bringing you coffee, she found herself continuing that little gesture for quite some time, even knowing you were gone.......

Often it's cold and lonesome out in that big old world and to know you have a mother to go home to occasionally means a lot. You said, "When I was working late at night and Hash kept Shane, it was the best feeling to come in so tired and cold and stay there some nights. It's weird driving home late at night and everything seems so lonesome on the road.

I'd go in and be real quiet and know Hash was in the bed in the other room and the little "bug" would be snuggled up warm and I'd crawl in beside him. That's the real feeling of home."

The next morning you would wake up and hear her "trying" to keep Shane quiet so you could sleep and often you'd hear her say to him: "I could wring your little neck!" Then, all too soon, that part of your life, and of ours, came to an end. Hash became sick and we were the ones looking in on her, checking to see if all was well and knowing it never would be, ever again.

You had gone out of the hospital briefly, just long enough to eat and then had peeked in her room about twelve o'clock to check on her. You recall that "She opened her eyes when I walked in, and looked surprised, so I told her I had just gotten off work and wanted to look in on her to see if she was OK. She didn't know I hadn't been able to work for days. I think she smiled and told me to go on home. I slept outside her room in a chair that night......that was the last time I saw her fully conscious. The morning before she died, I was sitting beside her bed and she opened her eyes once or twice for a second or two, but she didn't act like she saw me......."

You say your fondest memory is of her meeting you on the porch when you came back home after living with Lowell for a while; she hugged you and told you that you were her little girl and that she was glad you were home.

You remember that when she got all dressed up in something she liked "extra well" she'd be real prissy and kick one leg back behind her.

And when I asked you what picture comes to mind when you think of her, you said you see her in her robe, dancing around the floor to the music of the record player.

So always remember her that way—see her laughing and dancing—and remember that you shared much of that with her. And you can do it again.

# 19
## OBSERVATIONS ON A HAZELNUT

Unanimously, those who knew her would agree that she was indeed a Hazelnut!

She had a finely honed sense of humor—a sense of the ridiculous. Even though others were a part of her humor, no one was ever the "butt" of her jokes. That was something she taught me, and I in turn taught Scarlett and Tracy: Never make unkind cutting remarks about another human to get a laugh. That can leave scars that seem to be healed but never really are.......

My proudest moments have come when I have seen Scarlett or Tracy show kindness to another person, a person who deserves kindness.

She didn't take herself seriously and didn't expect anyone else to either, with one exception—when she was "witnessing" to them. Then she was strictly business, striving to put across every important point; that was her life.

She carried a perpetually puzzled look. How familiar we all were with that quizzical look—that air of confusion. Also, she was trusting and gullible, like a child. I told her so many, many tales that she fell for every time. Now Tracy does me exactly the same way, time after time. Each time I think I'll be prepared for his next story, but when the time comes, he tricks me again.

Once, with a completely straight face, Gadie told Hash that you could tell the age of a pig by the curls in its tail. One little curl meant six months, two curls meant a year and so on. She believed it wholeheartedly, and a year or so later I heard her telling someone that same story.

When it came to directions, she was at a complete loss. She had absolutely no sense of direction and I am my mother's child.

We were in Cynthiana one day with a group of friends and she was trying to find where a certain lady lived. The lady who answered the door and obviously lived there was not who she expected. She had the street and house number correct—what could be wrong? Throwing up her hands as she realized her mistake, she tossed a casual explanation over her shoulder to the astonished householder: "Sorry, wrong town!"

Can you imagine anyone never having a headache in their life? She said she never did, and that she often wondered what it would be like.

Also, she rarely got tired; she prided herself on that. So many times I have heard her say, "Nothing gets tired except my face." Then she would comment how her face looked like it had worn out a dozen bodies!

However, she took excellent care of her skin all her life; when I used to kiss her goodnight when I was little I would always feel and smell her cold cream. Now the smell of Pond's cold cream brings it all back.

Something hilarious happened at the chiropractor's office one day. Luxuriating in the soothing warmth and motion that was being applied to her back, she asked, "OOOh, what is that?" When the chiropractor nonchalantly answered: "my hand," she almost got hysterical with laughter because she had envisioned it as some vibrating heat machine. So many times she repeated that later and it got funnier each time.

As she hurried past her bed one day, she hung her toe on the bottom corner of it and almost broke it—her toe, not the bed. Raging incoherently, she ended her tirade with the unforgetable words: "What's it doing in here anyway?"

She reveled in my excesses as if they were her own. She gloried in my moments of flamboyance, even spurring me on.

Even though she dared not do it herself, she delighted in my indulgences with food. The first time Gadie and I went to the seafood extravaganza—The Lobster Feast—now replaced by The New Orleans House—I literally tried some of "everything" there. There must be at least fifteen different varieties of seafood, fixed in various ways.

Oysters Rockefellow, curried shrimp, frog legs, crab meat, oysters on the half shells, boiled shrimp, scallops, shrimp gumbo, etc.—I had some of everything. Followed up with a "whole" lobster. I was fine. I enjoyed every bite. I was violently sick for the next two days. And Hash loved it—my Roman orgy!

We don't realize the sadness and stress that people are concealing; it's all around us. Speaking of the New Orleans House reminds me of a fine person who works there—Trudy. Empathy, meaning emotional identification, draws people together in moments of relived grief: it helps to know others have suffered the same loss and to speak of it. Trudy lost her father a year ago and she still can't accept it. He was sixty-three, the same age as Hash, and he just "wore out." Various factors make acceptance of death harder; in Trudy's case it was the fact that she was a "Daddy's girl"........

I bought an outlandish black fur hat that towered high in the air above my head. The fact that it was so outrageous delighted Hash to no end and she encouraged me to wear it often.

Then I bought her one that was a scaled down version of mine and she loved it! It was black and furry and she looked like a little "polywog." She wore it constantly until it got too "ratty."

I never remember ever being cold but I know Hash must have expected to be one winter because she broke up the kitchen chairs and stuck them in the potbellied stove to keep the fire going. You might say she was agitated that time and that might be an understatement. I look back at this with genuine amusement and I relate it as the classic it is: Hash, breaking up the last chair with a vengeance, raises her fist to the heavens and says, "I hope when I die I go to a place where it is warm!"

How we laughed about that in later years. She laughingly denied that she ever said such a thing, but Mary Ann and I remember it, don't we?

In retrospect, I realize that her life was much harder than I have painted it. I'm sure that she had "her hands full" with five children and not much help; there must have been moments of pure desperation. I remember one—one that was repeated several times over the years.

Now it is funny and we laughed about it with her often in later years; back then it was not funny at all.

Reaching the end of her rope at the end of a frustrating day called for drastic measures, and this little incident reveals her firey nature. She would slam out of the back door into the darkness after announcing to one and all that she was going to take the axe and go out and kill herself! Can you imagine? Even though none of us really feared for her life, I did wonder at the time how Daddy could sit there and calmly read his book.

Actually, can't each of us understand the simple need she must have had at the time to escape the squabbling of five kids and the overpowering, endless household duties she faced?

I'm sure she went out into the warm quiet darkness (it was never winter when this happened) and had a smoke. She was a character and often added those touches of drama; they did emphasize the point!

Now Mary, I can remember the axe story well, but the story about her and the poker—you must be kidding!!

Of course, she was a spoiled young woman as no one disputes, who exchanged that pampered life for one with no luxuries and not even all the necessities. It was to be expected that she have her volatile moments; she deserved them.

Being headstrong and determined, she often did things her way if no alternative presented itself. She thought nothing of starting a long walk to town or to Momma's if she wanted to go and no one would take her. The angry "steam" she would build up inside at the circumstances would be sufficient to propel her for several miles. The fact that she would also be carrying a baby was of no importance either; she prided herself greatly on her stamina.

Poppa gifted her with a baby pig once when we lived at Mommau's and she raised it to be a fat hog.

Then came the day Poppa was taking his hogs to market to sell and Hash wanted to sell hers at the same time. She had plans for that money! But there was no one to help her and no way to get her hog down to Poppa's truck and she evidently didn't want to admit this to Poppa or to ask him to come after it. Therefore she again showed her "pioneer woman" spirit by walking ahead of that hog with an ear of corn in her hand, thus leading it along like that for two and a half miles! Straight to Poppa's truck before it left for the market—"Hell or a high stepping hog" never deterred her. She needed that money!

"Oh, isn't it amazing what a clever woman can do with a needle!" That's one of her famous observations; she was applying it to herself. Actually, all she could do with a needle was a neat hem or a quick button job, but she loved to say the above words.

"It's good stuff, but it'll rot!" That was a silly quotation from a book she read, and when she would feel the material on a new dress of mine, she would say that.

As mentioned elsewhere, she loved shoes, especially red shoes. She had a pair of white platform heels she especially liked; the extra inches added to her five foot four inch frame helped considerably. I can recall her exuberant attitude as she exclaimed: "When I mount those shoes, I feel ready for anything!"

"Oh, *why* am I so earthy?" This is another one of her famous sayings; she would throw her arms up in the air and ask the above question. I believe she got the idea from one of her favorite books—"The Good Earth" by Pearl Buck. Earthiness was her trademark—she gloried in it. In looking back, I realize many of the things she loved revealed this trait: Moon Drops make-up, Wind Song perfume, April Showers talc, etc.

She admired wild freedom and graceful movements. Momma and Bubble would come to spend the day with us when we lived up behind Kay's house, and they would be carrying a large basket between them, full of goodies. I remember streaking to meet them, happy and excited, and Hash admiringly said I looked just like a wild young deer.

Did any of you ever go off and forget your child somewhere? Hash did. I don't remember where it was, but on the way home she suddenly exclaimed: "Oh, I forgot the baby!" What I wonder about is why no one else noticed it either!

Back then, Hash had no tolerance whatsoever for liquor. She resented the beer and whiskey Daddy brought in, and never being a woman to suffer in silence, one day her resentment erupted into action. Upon opening the refrigerator door, she jerked every can of beer out, opened them all and thereupon proceeded to make good her threat to "drink every one of them"— until Daddy's interception on the first one. Her reasoning was that there must be something absolutely marvelous about this brew so why shouldn't she find out just what it was? Of course her abhorrence of the taste allowed her only a taste or two, but she made her point!

Have you ever had a "living bra?" Hash had one which she wore for years and years, and she said she finally had to beat it to death!

"Oh Lord, why couldn't I have been born *rich* instead of so beautiful?" She said that often over the years, laughing all the while.

She enjoyed her little glass of sherry every night; it helped her to sleep. Once, we said something to her about maybe giving it up—did she really need that or some such comment. In mock terror she was heard to exclaim: "I gave up my cigarettes, they want to take away my wine—next they'll be telling me that I can't have SEX!!"

She could act like she didn't have "a lick of sense," as she liked to point out at times. I like to see people laugh at themselves and have fun and she had her share.

In looking back over her life then, I see it as spiced with love and laughter—two very important ingredients for a balanced life.

Even though there were many times when the sounds of laughter and happiness were silenced, all in all she had her fair share and perhaps more than her share of fun and laughter. That is altogether fitting because, as the Bible says, "There is a time to laugh." And she enjoyed those moments to the fullest.

So in piecing together some of those moments, I can truly say that she was indeed a Hazelnut!

# 20
# ALWAYS A LADY

It's important for a woman to be a loving mother, a faithful wife and a trusting friend, but it seems to me that these qualities are more enhanced if along with them she is also a "lady." Being a "woman" is not synonymous with being a "lady."

There are, of course, cases where this desired quality is cultivated but more so it is an inborn thing, a special blessing and easily recognizable.

Hash was a lady. I'm proud that she was.

A lady deserves special attention; men don't tell dirty jokes in her presence. She handles life's situations in the best way available to her and she adapts to whatever her lot in life might be.

Often she told me that such and such a thing was not "ladylike." The word ladylike means refined and she admired refined people and taught me to.

Even the tone of a voice denotes this quality. I remember her speaking distastefully of some woman's "big coarse voice." Remember how she hated women's voices on James' C.B. radio?

Years ago she mentioned to me that she knew Alice was "growing up" because she had started lowering her voice when she talked.

We were taught, by example, not to use vulgar words and in fact, to be abhorrent of such words.

This is not to say that certain "spicy" words are to be avoided altogether. Sometimes the situation or a conversation is enhanced greatly by an appropriate word at the appropriate time. Certain words are at times deemed "necessary," and they don't have to knock the lady off the pedestal. A lady is not of necessity a prude!

Also, ladies don't run after boys! Let the boys run after you, but never ever do the running (or the calling). All female grandchildren—take note. It is good to be somewhat aloof and detached in such situations—at least it's different!

One time she told me about being in a movie and hearing a boy tell a girl he had his eye on to "come on down here with me." The girl replied, "You come up here with me." That made such an impression on Hash— evidently it did on me too since I remember it so vividly after all these years.

The point I am stressing now is that it certainly is refreshing to see a young lady be "hard to get" in these times of "easy come—easy go."

Hash wasn't always this modest as I might be leading you to believe. One "shining" example is the time she was seated on the platform at the meeting. She was taking part in a demonstration of a Bible study and was supposed to sit there and listen attentively. However, her chair was dangerously close to the edge. She made an unfortunate movement, the chair tipped over, and alas, she was thrown into a most "unladylike" position!

Did she regret her total lack of grace? Did she utter some gracious words to redeem her dignity? No, I'm sorry to report that her words to us later were pure vulgarity. She said: "Oh, I'm just glad I didn't have my other girdle on—the one without a crotch!"

She always looked her best when she went out; she never just ran out without "fixing up." That is something to be admired in a woman, isn't it? Have a sense of pride; be the best you can be.

I would be so proud I could hardly stand it when she was a substitute teacher at school and she would teach my class.

She was always stylish. Some women have it—some don't. She always had it. So many people were amazed to hear that she was sixty three when she died. (How I hate that word—how I despise death.) She truly looked and acted many years younger.

Many things contributed to that illusion: The glint in her eye, the quickness of her step and the cock of a hat....

Speaking of hats, she could certainly do justice to them. I gave her that brown felt hat she wore so often—the one with the brim turned just so. She really seemed to glow when she wore that hat.

Recently I was in a shop in Lexington, browsing through the dresses, when I spotted a display of hats. It actually hurt my heart when I saw the jaunty little hats, some with feathers, some with turned up brims, and I had to turn away, with tears in my eyes. Had she been alive I would surely have bought one for her; little hats made her happy...

In a partly serious way and partly joking she might also have been called a "woman of passions." She would have loved that; how she would have laughed.

But she only showed a passion for the things she really cared for; in all other things she was quite lackadaisical.

She had no desire whatsoever to move to any other house, no matter how grandiose it might promise to be. Being truly content with where she was seemed odd to me, but she sincerely was and often said she would never want to move from her friendly little house.

Speaking of her passionate nature reminds me of the song she used to laugh and laugh at. It was soon after she and James married and we lived at East Main. The song title escapes me, but this little man sang about making "mad passionate love" in a tinny little voice and it was hilarious.

Two other songs were popular then and I can just hear the titles and have a flood of memories. They were "He's Got the Whole World in His Hands" and one that had the words: "after I've given you the rainbow, I'll go out and I'll buy you the moon." She never gave up on James' promise to "buy her the moon." She always laughingly said he promised and she was still expecting it.

How she loved red shoes! She said "Every woman should have a pair of red shoes." She always had them—you bought her last pair for her, didn't you Mary? You used to tease her about getting rid of all those high heels and getting a pair of "Old Mother Comforts." You teasingly told her she needed to get into some sensible shoes and act her age. She really got a "kick" out of that every time, didn't she?

You know, I find a great deal of satisfaction in the fact that she never did have to "dismount" from her fancy shoes and wear older shoes.

When we lived on the hill and she first started working at the college, she bought herself a purple curduroy fitted dress with her pay. With it she wore red shoes, and that seemed such a daring combination then. She carried it off with style and I just recently saw a picture of her in that outfit.

Red shoes bring to mind the "passion" she had for a red slip. (Shades again of "Gone With the Wind.") She said a red slip made her feel very special; a woman should feel special if she wants to. Knowing that, you can appreciate this very personal bit of information.

When we three girls were looking through her closet, making the poignant choice of what she should be buried in, we came across her red slip. Looking at each other, we wordlessly agreed with our eyes—she should wear it. We felt it was altogether fitting and I think she would have smiled...no, she would have laughed—wickedly.

Kindness was a trait of hers and one she wanted us all to have. Kindness to people—and to animals. Her kindness and concern to animals that I mentioned elsewhere was also a fault to a certain extent. Scarlett also has that "fault" and I remember that Jeanne Tyson also was "overly concerned" with kindness to animals.

Haven't all of you heard the story of Glenne pushing Jeanne in the stroller when she was tiny and running over an ant with the stroller wheel? Jeanne had a fit and from then on waged her war against cruelty to poor animals. Do you remember her big dog named Panda?

To sum it up then, she was a conglomeration of personalities, as aren't most all mothers? We have to be to cope, don't we?

She was concerned, though somewhat vague; sometimes dissatisfied, sometimes content; mischievous in a naive way, plus many other things, but most of all and above all—she was always a lady!

# 21
# REFLECTIONS
## AND RECOLLECTIONS

There is a certain warm "smugness" that mothers and daughters have when they are close. It is something they exude unconsciously and others envy it. Hash and I had that—Scarlett and I have it too.

It is communicated by a certain appreciative glance, it is a special camaraderie and a satisfied comfortableness at being together. It's a word unspoken—a thought shared—a common goal.

I took it for granted with Hash, yet I appreciated it often; with Scarlett I strive for it constantly while trying to be nonchalant at the same time so as not to deter it.

Now I see the special "motherhood thing" with other mothers and daughters, like I used to have and I catch myself looking back—remembering that wonderful privilege. At times, I will be watching other mothers and daughters and I catch that wistful longing look of my Peter Pan picture on my face...

I would come to the meeting and if she was already there, I would slip into the seat beside her, or maybe somewhere else, and always she would give me a special approving look that spoke volumns.

Often she told me that I was a "great comfort" to her.

When I would take her home, she would often caution me to be sure and drive home carefully. We had a little joke about Gabriel, the guardian angel. She said she always sent him along with me in the car and when I would leave and no one else was in the car with me she would laugh and say, "You all be careful now."

Then she would always wave—always. Mary Ann and Alice and I never left until she got to the window inside and waved goodbye.

I couldn't believe it when she got to the point that she couldn't come to the window to wave. How could that be? I couldn't accept that, so when that happened, after leaving her house I would go to the outside of the window and wave in to her. She would smile and wave back.

Now when I go by her house I stare at that empty window and I wouldn't be surprised to see her there waving to me...I wave if there is no one in the car to see me acting so silly.

Now we do the same with Bubble. How would we have ever made it without her? She is the closest thing to Hash we could ever have—she looks and acts a lot like her.

After the funeral, she remarked that she had to hold up and carry on because "Now I have five children that need a mother..." How I have appreciated her loving care and just the fact that she is there to call and talk to. Just being there means so much.

Uncle Pal came by a few days ago and brought a little yellowed card he had been carrying in his wallet for forty-five years! I assume he has changed wallets several times. It was Hash's graduation card and on it was printed:

Hazel Betty Robertson
Georgetown, Kentucky, Route 2
Phone: 7102

Uncle Pal remembered that phone number—one of the first phones to be put in, in that part of the county. I remember an old crank phone on the wall at the store, but it was a later phone and not that one.

Speaking of the first phone reminds me of the fact that Poppa ran the first electricity lines into Muddy Ford too. He rounded up a group of local men who would be benefited from this, and they all labored together, free of charge, to get the job done. Momma cooked big meals for all of them, and soon the magical electricity was a part of their lives.

In the Bible, in the book of Judges, chapter twelve, there is a story about 42,000 Ephraimite men who were killed because they could not pronounce a word right. They were fighting against God's people and when they were defeated they tried to escape through the lines by pretending not to be Ephraimites. To determine whether or not they were, the men of Gilead would ask them to pronounce the work "shibboleth." They would attempt it, but for them it always came out "sibboleth."

All of us kids and a very few close relatives and friends can pronounce "Hash" the right way; all the others say "Hash," as in "turkey hash." Even Gadie has never been able to say it right and isn't that strange? In retrospect I can think of no one except the children and the grandchildren who could pronounce it right.

Memories are the glue between the past and the present. I love the month September because it rhymes with "remember." I'll never forgive Tracy for not holding off for two more days before being born—then he would have been a September baby instead of a nondescript August baby! (Perhaps he'll say I should have been the one to have held off.)

"How are things in Glocamora? Does that little stream still run through Glocamora?" How I remember her singing that and in fact, that song and "You Are My Sunshine" are the only two songs that I remember her caring for. I wanted to name the farm "Glocamora" so people could ask me, "How are things in Glocamora?" I guess I'll always be a silly dreamer...One time, Mary, you said to me: "I bet you even think you always look like you do when you look in your lighted makeup mirror!" And to my surprise I realized that yes, I did think that!

I was about twelve years old and down at Momma's, where I loved to be. Uncle Zip was so good to me; I guess I reminded him of his Shelia. He would go to the store and bring me those orange cupcakes and he would slip me a quarter often. I thought so much of him—he was a good man.

Uncle Russell and Aunt Ethel came down and brought a friend with them—I believe her name was Mary. She looked at me and said; "My God, what a head of hair!"

Momma handed me a Watchtower and tried to impress on me the importance of reading it as she looked at me intently with her little black eyes: "Now you read this—they're the best people in the world!" And I went out on the porch and sat in the swing, pretending to read...

Shirley would come walking in at Momma's with a pretty sweater and skirt on, eating a lemon and drinking a coke! I really thought she was "it" and I followed her every step she took. I must have worried her to death, but never once did she let on. She always called me "Fannee Gayle."

When she was small and sassy, she sashayed up to Lowell and mockingly said: "Lowell Scott called Sanny Gayle Panny Gayle!"

I remember "the coincidence of the pearls" and sometimes I think Hash was there and sometimes I'm not so sure. We were eating oysters at a restaurant and Tracy bit down on a pearl! We were so excited; we envisioned a perfectly developed pearl to dazzle one and all. Alas, we will never know how dazzling it might have been because as he took it from the oyster, he dropped it and it fell beneath the table. No problem, you say, to locate it? Well, unbelievingly, under that table was a broken strand of pearls! Hundreds of pearls, of all sizes! Imitation pearls to be sure—thereby making "our pearl" as a "pearl among swines." It was impossible to even try to locate it. Can you believe it—such a coincidence!

Being a proud woman, she was naturally conscious of the aging process and she worked at offsetting it as much as possible. Face creams, facial exercises, bodily exercises, experimenting with makeup and new styles—like us, she tried them all. I saw an advertisement for a face band to be worn tucked under the hair; it was supposed to take years off your face. Giving her the ad, I awaited her opinion of it; I would probably have bought it for her. A few days later, she said she didn't think she would be interested in it because, as she said: "I have seen too many old ladies make fools of themselves when they got to thinking they were young again." I thought no more of it until we were looking through the drawer where she kept pictures and other things of importance to her. She kept such a very few things, but there, tucked away among her personal thing was that little advertisement...

Hash had faults, of course, and she'd be the first one to tell you so. In regard to us, I would say the fact that she didn't push us any, gave us no real goals and no sort of training was her main shortcoming. That has made it hard on us and we can see and feel the effects—we weren't really taught much. We just drifted along and that's no good—you have to learn sooner or later, and sooner is so much better. The only thing I can really remember her taking the time to teach me was how to iron those puffed sleeves in little girl's dresses.

Mary Ann, you remember her telling you these all-important words: "If you ever drop macaroni on the floor, pick it up right then or it will get mashed and be hard to get up."

Also, she taught us not to speak of unpleasant things during a meal—to save them until later so as not to interfere with the all-important digestion.

Other than that, I can't remember any specific training and her lackadaisical approach to that all-important task is what I consider her greatest fault. That in itself can accomplish something if it spurs us on to avoid the same mistakes.

When you have a mother, you are still a child, regardless of your age; losing her makes you feel so much older. I see people who are much older, even in their sixties, who still have their mothers and I feel resentment—I feel deprived. We shouldn't have lost her—it wasn't right.

I appreciated having her. I appreciate having Daddy. When we would leave town, as we often did and still do, I would pass Bubble's street and wave a mental goodbye; I would pass Etta Lane and do the same; likewise at Daddy's road. Even then I felt blessed at having them there, knowing they would be there when I returned...

Hash didn't seem to have any sense of continuity; she seemed quite unconcerned with the past and the future. I can't understand that—I who am so absorbed with both, perhaps too much so. She didn't want to be hampered even whatsoever with nonessentials; this included momentos and souvenirs of the past.

Knowing this, I was taken by surprise to hear from you, Alice, that she had recorded our names and birthdates in one of her Bibles. Nothing elaborate, mind you, but the fact that she had done that surprised me greatly.

When I was starting to grow and my legs were getting longer and "skinnier," before I caught up with them, she laughingly called them "twa sticks."

How proud she would have been recently to hear what an examination revealed about Mary Ann and about Scarlett. The person doing the examining made this observation on both of them: "You are from really 'good stock;' you have very few inherited weaknesses!" She loved the idea of "good stock"—that is something she passed on to us and how thankful I am of that!

I hope you have enjoyed these recollections; they're only several out of a great collection I have stored in a safe place—in my mind.

Perhaps they have helped to present a better understanding of a many-faceted woman—which she was.

# 22
# NEVER FORGET TO REMEMBER

For almost two years now I have worked on this book; for that amount of time I have kept her alive in my mind. Very much alive. I have recalled her words, relived her past and sought to give meaning to events that led to her death. Having analyzed, devised and revised all that I can, it is now near completion.

I have lived with this book day and night; it has never been far from my mind. In the middle of a conversation, I might latch on to a word or a phrase being used and while seemingly still tuned in to the conversation, I would be at work incorporating that phrase into a certain chapter.

When anyone spoke of her, I memorized every word—could it be new material for me to use?

Supposedly without her knowledge, I picked Bubble's mind for details, dates, and family history. I quizzed Daddy and Kay relentlessly on rememberances and anecdotes. I recorded conversations, I dug through old cedar chests and I invaded your memories. In doing so, I feel I have presented an accurate picture of Hash. It will be a word picture that we can all refer to when we have the need to, a memory bank to rely on. It is my memorial to her and my way of thanking her for all she was to me.

During this time I have constantly played with words and thoughts and have been obsessed with sentences. My very being has been involved with the completion of this book.

Now I understand why they say writers are absent-minded and preoccupied and why they have a certain distant air about them. I understand, because all of this time I have been immersed in the pages of this book even when I should not have been.

So now, as it nears completion, I begin to worry how I will feel when I am through; not only do I worry, indeed I fear how I will feel. This has kept her alive and each day has perpetuated her memory, in necessity to the work. Will I feel empty and drained, as perhaps you do, having had nothing to spur you on?

Constantly my memories have been revived, churned up as though by one of those ancient fans that hang from the ceiling, lazily revolving my mind, never ending...thus necessitating a cataloging of my remembrances —lest I forget.

Writing the book has been like having a baby; there are many similarities. The idea was first "conceived" soon after she died. As it "grew" inside of me, I thought of little else. I made plans for it: How to introduce it to the world and what it's "name" would be. I wondered how it would be accepted...would it be "big" enough to encompass all the dreams and ideals I had poured into it?

There is one thing wrong, however, with this idea of me as the "mother" of the book—the husband is usually in on a surprise of this sort, but in keeping it a secret from all of you, I also kept it a secret from Gadie!

That was hard to do, but I felt a great need to keep it to myself—to show that I could do something entirely on my own...

I am so very grateful for Gadie's patience and great understanding as he gave me the freedom to do what I had to do, even though he didn't know what it was. He just knew it was very important to me...

First the notebooks were filled, page by page, with the words I had inside me. The words were then transferred onto tape; the voice was heard. The voice—careful to show no emotion because emotions are not shown by "ladies"—be calm and composed at all times.

The the tapes were converted to the printed page—typed painstakingly and for undertaking such an "ordeal" and doing a fine job in the process, I want to thank Wilma Childers. How she ever endured all my starts and stops and back-ups and flash-backs, I'll never know, but she managed to "follow" and transfer my words onto paper. I am very grateful.     I also want to thank Judy Butcher for so graciously offering to do the tedious job of typing the manuscript, but distance and deadlines made my acceptance of her assistance impossible.

And now, soon, my book's "birth" will be proclaimed to all the family. It will be "laid open" to public scrutiny—to open and close at will.

Soon now it will be "expelled" and I will feel a great surge of relief; it is what I have been looking forward to for so long. Now, as "the birth" draws near, I am filled with trepidation; can it possibly turn out to be all that I have expected it to?

I keep looking back. A certain day comes to mind almost every time I pass Etta Lane...having spent a day shopping in Lexington, we rode home together on the bus, this being before I learned to drive. Getting off first, at Etta Lane, she tossed me a smile and a wave as I looked out the window and then I went on alone. We had shared a fine day, with no regrets, but as the bus pulled away, I kept looking back...

We'll always be looking back, won't we? This book can serve as a guide, but actually, when we want to remember, all we have to do is close our eyes...I can close my eyes and come up with the most marvelous picture of her—a composite picture—by putting together the assorted memories I have gleaned from you, her children...she is waving her hands and "preaching," eager to get across a point, but she takes out time to dance the Charleston before she rushes into the kitchen, doing whatever she can to please us, and afterwards she sits down for a minute to read, and through it all, she's smiling.

We should smile too, in remembrance; it's what she would have wanted. For years, before there was ever a hint of trouble, I have heard her say this numerous times: "If anything should ever happen to me, don't *ever* grieve for me!"

To punctuate this, the final chapter, I would like to insert a little word picture of her which is my favorite.

Before going up to her porch, she would often look back over her shoulder at me, tossing her head and rolling her eyes, as she kicked up her heel in a sassy way.

That's the way I want to remember her—that's the way she'll look again.

In summation then, I want to tell you the meaning of the word "remember." It means "to be careful not to forget."

Now as we go our separate ways through life, the ways will often be lonely, so do what you will, do what you must, but above all, make sure you never forget to remember the mother we called Hash...

# 23
# AS THE DAYS OF A TREE

I look at life as a tree and
to me it is quite simple.
We do both start out as a seed
you see and none will disagree.
At the very start, when we
first struggle for life, as babies
will do, we are the same as a
frail young sprout pushing
thru the soil-gasping for light and
air.
From there, if nourished and cared
for properly, we develop into a
sturdy young sapling.
Coming into the seasons of
our life—looking always upward
for our source of life—we are the same.
Depending upon our creator—arms
reaching outward—we grow straight
and tall...Hopefully.
The spring of our life is tender and
we are oh so vulnerable!
So much depends on our
environment and on love. We begin
to blossom and put out tiny
feelings to the world—Always
hesitant, yet eager to burst

forth at the first encouragement.
     Some will make it—some will
not. The tragedy of life is that many
wilt and die...never to leave their
silhouette against a perfect sky.
Were their roots not persistent—were
the desires not strong? Spring will tell.
     Now summer—we are full-blown
and confident! Insecurities and timidity
are not for us—we will last
forever! Ripe and satisfied, we bask
in the high noon of our achievements...
This is all we need.
We are self-sufficient and secure.
After all, consider our tap—root!
Nothing is impossible—our tree tops
reach high and are laden with
our gains—our leaves will never fall!
     But alas! What is this! A
tinge to our green! A silver hair!
No Way! That can't be true! Not to
us—the vibrant king of the forest!
     Then quite by surprise, Jack
Frost, Old Age Himself, slips in
by cover of night and touches
us with a maturity we never
requested nor wanted. Slowly at
first, against our will, but gradually
accepted, we see our leaves turn
to hues that are really quite
beautiful. In time we welcome
our new found change...even
happily embrace it because we have
reached the fullness of our life
and now can't we and all around
us see that maturity is the most
glorious time of all? Isn't it?
     So we are allowed to bask in
it and to reflect it all around
us. Others enjoy it too...The woods
are alive with smiles of sunshine.
Our deeds of love and kindness
crackle beneath their feet—bringing
glorious shades of happiness to be
appreciated.
     But wait..What is this? We seem
to have lost our grip on our

surroundings! Day by day we begin
to lose something, it seems...A
chill prevades the forest. Day by day—
Leaf by leaf—we can sense the
approaching time...Of what? Why
am I so afraid? Why?

Now it is upon me and I
understand. My time is past—winter
has fallen. I no longer feel the
sun...I no longer hear the birds.

But why is it to be—Must
it be my time? Only a little
while more—I have so much to do!

But it is not to be—I feel
the sudden white stillness descend
upon me, leaving me stiff and
quiet. So very quiet.

Reflecting upon my seasons
now past, I wonder: Was I
loved—Am I missed—Why
did I not do more?

So life is over and all
is done and to you I bid
fare-well...Forever...

Hark! What is that tiny
stirring so deep within me?
What is that far away glimmer
I catch? Can it be? Is it really
so?? Yes—Yes!! I—I who
loved life..*I* will live again!

# About the Author

Fannee Hilander's *Hold Back The Spring* is now in its second printing and she continues to celebrate "All Things Kentucky" by means of her writing and filmmaking. She welcomes your support for Kentucky by emailing her at – indiansummerproductions@yahoo.com

Cover photo restoration and back cover photo By John S. Hockensmith